more

Joe's

Jokes

A Minister's Mirth

Volume Two

An anthology of tall tales and humorous stories suitable
for numerous occasions. The profits of this book are for the
work of the Irish Mission of the Presbyterian Church in Ireland

Published by Burning Bush Publications
134, Ballynahinch Road, Lisburn, Co. Antrim BT27 5HB

Copyright Notice

Humorous Stories
For Various Occasions

Dear Reader of Joe's Jokes,

If you have read Volume One of Joe's Jokes, I expect you are among the 5,000 plus who have looked forward to Volume Two. The sale of the first volume passed all our expectations, proving that the Public, who have a good sense of humour, appreciate a book that contains jokes which will not offend and which can be told in any company. Again there are more than 300 humorous stories or jokes which are waiting to be told person to person, or to an audience, or even as you relax in a chair or lie in your bed. People love to laugh and who doesn't need to laugh these days?

As in Volume One, here are stories about Ministers, Weddings, for After Hospitality, Miscellaneous and not least numerous Irish jokes. This is the promised Second Volume which the Public has often enquired about. I trust it will be as well received and go round the world like its predecessor. The profits of these little Joke books go to help the work of the Irish Mission.

Thank you for your support.

J. B. Mooney

CONTENTS

TALES ABOUT CLERGYMEN

71. OLD BLETHER
A retired Minister was invited to preach at an Evening Service and he took his wife along with him.

Minister to wife: "You just go in at the front door and take a seat, and I'll go round to the Minister's room".

Elder to wife: "You are most welcome to our Church. I hope you'll enjoy the service".

He was not aware that she was the visiting Minister's wife.

Elder after the Service to wife: "I hope you will come back again. You know, we don't have that old blether preaching every Sunday".

72. SHIRT BUTTON
The Minister preached in a Church which was looking for a new Minister, but he was not successful. A Colleague asked him, "What went wrong you didn't receive a 'Call' to that Church you preached for?".

Minister: "It was all my own fault. I always put a little sweet under my tongue which lasts twenty minutes. When it is dissolved, I know it is time to stop talking. Unfortunately, I had preached for nearly an hour before I realised I had put a shirt button under my tongue by mistake".

73. PRISON CHAPLAIN
Colleague: "Why did you appoint the Rev. Bogg to the post of Prison Chaplain? He is the last fellow I would have thought suitable".

Bishop: "I chose him for the job because he emptied the last three Churches he was in".

74. NEW PRISON CHAPLAIN
On conducting his first Religious Service as Prison Chaplain, he made the mistake of saying, "I'm glad to see so many here today, it is most encouraging!".

75. ADAM

Minister to boy: "Can you tell me who lived in the Garden of Eden?".
Boy: "I think it was the Adamses".

76. CUT CHIN

John: "I see the Minister has a small plaster on his chin. Did he cut himself?".
Willie: "Yes, he said while he was shaving he was concentrating on his Sermon and he cut himself".
John: "Well, in future, he should concentrate on his shaving and cut his Sermon".

77. CAN I CHEW?

A man had never been in Church in his life, but a friend persuaded him to attend. In Church the following conversation took place:
Man: "Can I smoke?".
Friend: "No, you can't".
Man: "Can I chew?".
Friend: "No, you can't".
But the man put a bit of chewing tobacco in his mouth.
Man: "Can I spit?".
Friend: "No, you can't".
Just then a man came down the aisle and handed him an empty collection plate.
Man: "You're too late mate. I've just swallowed it".

78. K.I.S.S.

The visiting Preacher noticed in the Pulpit where the Minister could see it, a card with the letters K.I.S.S. on it. At lunch in the Manse, he said to the Minister's wife, "You must be a very affectionate couple for I noticed the word 'K.I.S.S.' in the Pulpit where your husband could easily see it". The wife replied, "No, it is not what you think it means. It is a reminder to my husband regarding the sermon to 'Keep It Short, Sam'".

79. GIRL I LEFT BEHIND

The new Organist never played an appropriate piece of music as the Congregation was leaving the Church. The Minister said to the Organist, "I would like you to listen carefully to the Sermon and play something

appropriate as the people are leaving".
The following Sunday, the Minister preached on 'Lot's wife' and, to his consternation, the Organist began to play 'The girl I left behind'".

80. NOT FIT TO LIVE WITH PIGS
Sexton: "Tommy Brown was saying last night that you are not fit to live with pigs".
Minister: "And what did you say?".
Sexton: "Oh, I stuck up for you. I said you were".

81. PREACHING AND PRACTISING
Two bachelor brothers lived in the same house. One was a Doctor of Medicine and the other was Doctor of Divinity. A man called at the house one day and asked if the Doctor was in. The old house-keeper replied, "Is it the one who practises you want or the one who preaches?". The man replied, "I want the one who practices, please".

82. PRIEST TO HEAVY DRINKER
Priest: "If you don't stop drinking, I'll turn you into a mouse at midnight".
Later, the man went to bed, but kept looking at the clock.
Man to wife: "In about 15 minutes, if you see me getting smaller and smaller and grey fur covering me all over, get up quickly and put the cat out".

83. WAKEN HIM UP YOURSELF
Minister to Choir member: "You see that man over there going to sleep? I want you to give him a nudge and waken him up".
Choir member: "I think you should do it yourself, for you are the one who put him to sleep".

84. GIVING GOD CREDIT.
Some Christians are ready to give God credit, but they are very slow to give Him cash!

85. QUARE GUNK
The Minister called with a parishioner in the mid-afternoon. Before leaving, he suggested they have a word of prayer. The man of the house said, "Let's call John the gardener in, for he is a Church member". He tapped the window to call John in and remarked to the Minister, "He's going to get a

quare gunk, for he thinks he is coming in for his tea".

86. SERMONS IN EVERY BLADE OF GRASS
Minister to gardener: "Jack, I see you are cutting the grass around the Church".
Jack: "Yes, you said last Sunday that there is a sermon in every blade of grass, so I'm trying to keep them short".

87. DEAF MINISTER
Parishioner: "Our old Minister should be retired years ago. You know, he is so deaf, the last time he was in our house he knelt to say a prayer and the whole time he didn't realise he was kneeling on the cat".

88. CURATE AND NO PETROL
The young Curate was travelling along the Motor-way with his wife and child. When he ran out of petrol a motorist kindly stopped and offered to siphon some of his petrol to get him to the next Filling Station, providing the Curate had a can to put the petrol in. He had no can, but he said he would use the baby's potty and that would do just as well. As he was pouring the petrol into his car an A.A. man stopped and had a good look. He hesitated and then said, "I'm not a religious man, but I admire your faith."

89. NAGGING WIFE
Parishioner: "My wife is a holy terror the way she goes at me. She nags, nags, nags. Would you agree to come and speak to her?".
Minister: "If I can be of any help, I will come".
Parishioner outside door: "You wait here till I get her started"

90. FEEDING THE SHEEP
The visiting Minister turned up to preach one night when the snow was falling thick and fast. To his dismay, he found just one old farmer at the service.
Minister to farmer: "Seeing you are the only one present tonight would you rather I didn't preach a sermon?".
Farmer: "Go ahead and preach, for if I had only one sheep, I would feed it".
The Minister duly went ahead and preached a 30 minute sermon. On going out, the old farmer said to the Minister: "Yes, if I had only one sheep I would feed it, but I wouldn't give it enough to feed the whole flock".

91. BUSY MINISTER

Wife: "Take a day off: go and play a game of golf".
Husband: "What will you say if someone is looking for me?".
Wife: "I'll tell them you are away on a course!".

92. DRIP IN PULPIT

Minister, making announcements: "I'm pleased to report that the leaks in the roof have all been repaired. Unfortunately, there is still a drip in the Pulpit".

93. RADIO SERVICE

The Scotsman was listening to a Religious Service on the Radio. He appeared to be enjoying it, but when the Collection was announced, he got up and switched the Radio off!

94. MINISTER'S TONSILS

Parishioner to Doctor: "I hear our Minister is to have his tonsils out. Will he be able to preach after the operation?".
Doctor: "There is no doubt about it....he will be able to preach".
Parishioner: "Thank goodness, for up till now he can't preach for nuts".

95. PYJAMAS IN CHURCH

The small boy was taken to Church for the first time.
Father: "Close your eyes, son, the Minister is going to pray".
Boy: "He can't be, Daddy, for he hasn't got his pyjamas on".

96. LIQUOR IN THE RIVER

The Minister was giving a talk on the subject of "Temperance".
In his address, he said, "If I had my way, I would pour all liquor into the river".
He must have forgotten that remark, for when he finished his address, he announced, "Our closing Hymn is number 570, 'Shall we gather at the river?'".

97. BISHOPS' CONFERENCE

The Bishop went to the receptionist's desk and said, "I'm sorry, Miss, but I have a problem".
Girl: "Sir, we don't have problems in this Hotel, just opportunities".
Bishop: "Call it what you will, but there is a woman in my room".

98. GRACE BEFORE MEALS

Two men were crossing a field in which there was an angry Bull. As it was seen charging towards them, one man said to the other: "You go to Church; pray quickly".

Man: "I only know one prayer".

Companion: "Then say it quickly".

Man: "Lord, for what we are about to receive make us truly thankful".

99. RETIRING MINISTER

Minister to Parishioner: "I know I am leaving, but cheer up, you will probably get a better Minister when I go".

Parishioner: "Not necessarily, that is what the last one said before he left".

100. STICKING THE HEAT

The Minister had been away on holiday and he was unaware that a certain member of his Congregation had died during his absence. The widow of the man never forgave him for when they met in the street, the Minister asked, "How is your husband sticking the heat?".

101. LABOUR

When the lady Minister's first baby was expected, she was granted permission to 'labour within the bounds of the Presbytery'.

102. HOTEL NOT TALL ENOUGH

Minister arriving at Hotel: "How much are your rooms for the night?".

Receptionist: "First floor rooms are £50. Second floor rooms are £40. Third floor rooms are £30. As he turned to leave, the Receptionist asked, "Don't you like our Hotel?"

Minister: "Oh, it is a beautiful Hotel, but it just isn't tall enough".

103. JOHN IN HEAVEN

Minister to lady: "How is your husband?".

Woman: "Oh, John is in Heaven".

Minister (taken unawares) blurted out: "I'm sorry to hear that". Then realising he had said the wrong thing, he complicated it more by saying, "What I meant to say was I'm surprised".

104. PRODIGAL SON
Minister to Sunday School class: "When the Prodigal son returned home there was much rejoicing, but there was one for whom the feast brought no happiness. Can you tell me who that was?".
Boy: "Please, Sir, was it the fatted calf?".

105. HEAVEN
Tom came home from Sunday School crying. Mother: "Why are you crying?".
Tom: "The teacher asked all those who wanted to go to Heaven to put up their hand".
Mother: "Did you put your hand up?".
Tom: "No", he sobbed, "because you told me to come straight home".

106. MISSING INGREDIENT
The missing ingredient in most of our preaching is a little shortening.

107. DIDN'T KNOW WHAT SIN WAS
Woman to Minister as he was about to leave the parish for another Church, "We are going to miss you. I never knew what sin really was until you came".

108. TOO NEAR HEADQUARTERS
The Minister was on the plane when the Stewardess brought round the drink.
Stewardess: "What would you like, Sir?".
Minister: "Coca-Cola will do".
Stewardess: "Are you sure you wouldn't like something stronger?".
Minister: "No, I'm too near Headquarters for that".

109. NOT MISSING MUCH
Minister: "Mrs. Smith, I'm sorry you can't get out to Church these days".
Smith: "It is this arthritis I have in my knees that prevents me going".
Minister (modestly): "Maybe you are not missing much".
Mrs. Smith: "Maybe so, for that is what the people tell me".

110. FUNERAL CAR
The Minister was in the back seat of the Funeral Car on the way home from the Cemetery. He leaned forward and touched the driver on the shoulder.

This greatly startled the driver and the Minister apologised. "Oh, that's alright" said the driver. It is just that I usually drive the hearse!".

111. LOOSE LIVERS
At the Mid-week meeting a lady asked her Minister to pray for her sister's "floating kidney". "Well now," said the Minister: "I wouldn't like to do that in a public meeting".
Woman: "I don't see why not; last week you prayed for 'looselivers'".

112. HOLY WATER
The Priest who was crossing the Border between the North and South of Ireland had purchased some whiskey. At the Border he was confronted with the Custom's Officer.
Custom's officer: "Well, Sir, what have you in the bottle?".
Priest: "Holy water, Sir". The Officer unscrewed the cap of the bottle took one sniff and exclaimed, "I'm afraid this is no 'Holy Water', it is pure whiskey"
Priest: "Glory be! The age of miracles is not over yet".

113. IT DOESN'T MEAN A THING
Grandfather took his little grandson to Church for the first time. When an Elder entered the Pulpit with the Bible, the people stood up. "What does that mean?" he asked his grandfather. He replied, "It means that the Bible is central in worship". When the Minister held out his arms and said, "Let us pray", the boy asked what that meant. Grandfather said, "It is to get the people together for prayer". Just before the Minister preached, he took off his wrist watch and put it down beside him. "What does that mean?" asked the boy. "Son", said grandfather, "that doesn't mean a thing".

114. HOMER
The new baby was being baptised and the Minister was talking to the father.
Minister: "What is the baby's name?".
Father: "His name is 'Homer'".
Minister: "How unusual. I'm glad you are interested in the Classics".
Father: "That's not why we called him 'Homer'...I happen to be a pigeon fancier".

115. GOOD HOME FOR SPADE

The Minister who wasn't known for being energetic went in to a shop to buy a spade.

Shopkeeper: "I'm glad it is going to a good home. I know it won't be overworked!".

116. YES, FATHER

After the man-servant had done something stupid, he was rebuked by the Priest.

Priest (seeing a donkey in the field): "There's your brother over there".
Manservant: Yes, Father".

117. BUS 20

Visitor to town: "Sir, can you tell me which Bus to take for Stormont?".
Minister: "Yes, take Bus 20; the 20th Bus".

118. WONT BAPTISE OUR WEANS

The old age Pensioner went to his Minister in First Congregation to arrange a date for his wedding. The Minister said, "John, have a titter of wit...go home and forget about it". So John went to the Minister in Second Congregation and asked whether he would marry them and he readily agreed. The big day came and the two pensioners were duly married. As they were coming down the steps of the Church, John turned to his bride and said, "That man up in 'First' won't baptise any of our weans".

119 ASSISTANT

Assistant: "Sir, I would rather be called 'Associate Minister' rather than 'Assistant Minister'".

Senior Minister: "What difference does it make, anyhow? Sure they can both be abbreviated to Ass".

120. REND YOUR HEARTS

The Minister announced, "The offering last Sunday was £10.50 and two buttons. My text today is 'Rend your hearts and not your garments!'".

121. BETTER QUARTERS

The Presbyterian Minister visited the home of the local Parish Priest. On being shown around the house, the Minister remarked, "You certainly have good quarters here".

The Parish Priest replied, "I may have the better quarters, but you have the better half".

122. HORSE AND TRAP

The country people were mourning the death of Old Billy, who was known to all, but no more so than the Minister, for Old Billy had bought the horse and trap from him. The Minister had distinctly told Old Billy that he must shout "Hallelujah" if he wanted the horse to start and that he must shout "Amen" if he wanted it to stop. It so happened that Billy was out one day and they came to the edge of a cliff. At the last minute, Billy saw the danger and shouted "Amen". The horse duly stopped, but in his relief, Billy shouted "Hallelujah" and over the cliff they went.

123. LONG SERMON

The Minister had preached a rather long sermon and a dear old lady felt uncomfortable. As the Minister was shaking hands with the people going out, she whispered in his ear, "The head can take in only what the bum can endure".

124. BOGGIN (Irish word for dirty)

The new Minister, not used to the country, called at the farmhouse of a Parishioner. There was a pile of potatoes on the kitchen floor which they were cutting up for seed planting. The woman apologised and said, "You will have to excuse us, your Reverence, but you can see we are boggin". The Minister had never heard that word before and did not know its real meaning. He went to the next farm and saw the same thing taking place with all the potatoes on the floor. He offended the woman by saying, "I see you are like the Murphy's....you're boggin".

125. THREEPENCE IN THE OFFERING.

A well known Belfast Minister pleaded for a generous offering from his Congregation. When it was counted, he said, "The offering amounted to £350 and 3p. There must be a Ballymena man in the Congregation tonight." One man put his hand up and said, "There are three of us."

126. SPEECHES

The young Minister wrote to a famous orator and asked him for some advice as to how to preach and hold an audience. The orator wrote back, saying, "Start with something good. End with something good. And have very little in between".

127. TAPE RECORDER
The Minister thought it would be a good idea if he bought a Tape Recorder so that he could listen to his sermons on the Saturday night, so he purchased one. On Saturday night, having finished his Sermon for the next day, he put it on tape. He then sat back in his armchair to listen to the finished product. Unfortunately, he fell asleep half way through it!

128. MINISTER AND HIS WIFE (at Installation reception)
Tenders were asked for the building of the cross-channel tunnel. All were astronomically priced except one tender from an Irishman. When asked how he could do it for such a ridiculous amount, he replied, "My brother and I work together and we each have a pick, a shovel and a wheelbarrow. He will begin digging in France and I will begin digging in England and we will meet half way".
"But", said the interviewer, "What will happen if you don't meet half way?".
"Well", said the Irishman, "You'll have two Tunnels for the price of one!".

Application. With your new Minister and his wife, you have got two for the price of one.

129. CHURCH PILLARS
Minister: "There are two kinds of pillars in this Church:
      1. Pillars who hold up the Church.
      2. Caterpillars who crawl in and out".

130. PREACHER'S EXPENSES
The Church Treasurer was giving his Annual report and he announced that the Pulpit expenses paid to the Minister who was responsible for preaching during their own Minister's holiday, amounted to £120. One of the Committee members rose to his feet and said, "That's a ridiculous amount of money to pay. I watched the man as he preached and the only thing he drank was water!".

131. CHURCH TREASURER

When you think of a Treasurer, you naturally think of money. The School teacher said to her class, "Let us do some mental arithmetic this morning. John, if you had £1.50 in one pocket of your trousers and 75p in another pocket, what would you have?". John: "Please Miss, I would have somebody else's trousers on".

132. SQUEEZING THE ORANGE (For thanks to Treasurer)

The Strong man at the Side Show held up an orange in full view of his audience and said, "I am going to squeeze this orange of all its juice and, after having done so, I challenge anyone to come up and squeeze another drop out of it. In fact, if anyone can squeeze another drop out of it, I'll pay him £1 for each drop of juice he extracts. A number of men stepped forward and tried, but to no avail. It seemed as if the strong man had extracted the last drop.

Finally, another man stepped forward and took the orange in his hand. He held the audience spell-bound as he squeezed...one drop, two drops, three drops until he had squeezed five drops. The crowd roared and cheered. The strong man said, "If I hadn't seen it with my own eyes, I wouldn't have believed it". He asked the man the secret of his success. The man replied, "I'm the local Church Treasurer and the people say I could squeeze blood out of a stone".

Application. "I don't know whether it was due to the Treasurer's excessive squeezing or not, but while he has been our Treasurer, the giving has increased and, as he hands over to another, the books are in a very healthy state. Thanks".

133. ONLY ONE POTTY

The visiting Minister was asked to share the bedroom of the small boy in the house. As bedtime came around, the Minister saw the little boy kneel at the side of his bed. He thought he would encourage the boy by doing the same. He knelt down beside him.

Wee Boy: "What are you doing, Mister?".

Minister: "The same as you, John".

Wee boy: "You'll catch it from mother in the morning for there is only one potty and I'm using it".

134. FALSE TEETH

The bishop had arrived at the Church to confirm some young folk. He was in a terrible state. His new teeth were uncomfortable and he had taken them out. Now he discovered he had mislaid them. The Rector said to him, "Don't worry: there's no problem. I've a man in my congregation who can help you out". The man was contacted and, having produced a few sets, the Bishop found one to fit. "Oh," said the Bishop, "It is most fortunate that you have such a good dentist among your flock". "Actually", replied the Rector: "I'm afraid he is not a Dentist. He's the local Undertaker".

135. HAT IN CHURCH

The man entered the Church and sat with his hat on. Everybody noticed him, but nobody said anything to him. Eventually, one of the Elder's approached him and said it was not right for him to keep his hat on in Church. The man replied, "I have been coming to this Church each Sunday for six months and nobody ever spoke to me. At least, with wearing my hat I have managed to get one to speak to me".

136. SCREW UP THE WICK

The small preacher in the big pulpit gave out as his Text, "I am the Light of the world".
He repeated this a number of times and then one man in the congregation was heard to say, "Screw up your wick, I can't see you ".

137. HARDLY KNEW YOU

The lady was persuaded to attend Church after a lapse of time. It happened to be Easter Sunday and she bought a new outfit for the occasion. As she entered the Church, wearing her new clothes, the Choir was singing, "Hallelujah, Hallelujah". The woman walked out, saying she wouldn't be back. On being asked why? she replied, "Just because I had a new outfit on, the whole Choir started to sing, 'I hardly knew you: I hardly knew you'".

138. SOOTHING, MOVING AND SATISFYING

Professor to young Minister preaching for a Church: "Make sure your Sermon is soothing, moving and satisfying and you will have no difficulty."
Sad to say, he wasn't successful.
He said to the professor later: "I know my sermon was moving, for some people walked out. I know it was soothing, for some people nodded off to

sleep. I know it must have been satisfying, for I wasn't asked back".

139. HE MAKES ME BLUSH
Jane: "Do many people attend your Church ? " Mary: "No, in fact there so few that when the Minister says, "Dearly Beloved" he makes me blush."

140. WERE YOU IN THE ARK?
The Minister's grandson said, "Granda, were you in the Ark ? "
Minister: "No son, I wasn't in the Ark."
Boy: "Then why were you not drowned?"

141. SHORT POEM
> Every time I see a Church
> I pay a little visit
> So that when I'm carried in
> The Lord wont say, 'Who is it?'

142. ATTENTION IN CHURCH
First Minister: "Does it bother you if folk in the congregation look at their watch while you are preaching?"
Second Minister: "No, but what bothers me is when they put their watch to their ear to see if it is still going."

HAPPILY EVER AFTER

36. UMBRELLA
The Commercial traveller had vacated his room in the Hotel and a Honeymoon couple had moved in. Unfortunately, he forgot his umbrella and returned to the room to get it. When he came to the door, he heard voices.
Bridegroom: "Darling, your eyes are all mine; your ears are all mine and your lips are all mine".
Traveller: "Well now, when you come to the umbrella, it's mine" .

37. WON'T TURN
The Porter in the Hotel reported to the Manager that the newly married couple who had just arrived, were behaving in a very peculiar way. In fact, on the two occasions when he entered their room with luggage, they were standing back to back. The Manager decided to investigate.
Manager: "Is there something wrong in that you are both standing back to back? " .
Bridegroom: "Mary is a Roman Catholic and I am a Protestant and neither of us will agree to turn".

38. LAST WORDS
Tom: "I hear old John died last week. He was always a quiet man .... I wonder what his last words were?" .
Jack: "He didn't have any last words for his wife was with him until the last".

39. CLOTHES WON'T FIT HER
John' s wife was on her death-bed and John sat by her side .
Martha: "I want you to promise me two things before I leave you. The first is that you will look out for a nice woman and marry again" .
John: "If that's what you wish, then I'll promise. What is the second thing you want me to promise to do?".

Martha: "The second thing I want you to promise is that she will wear none of my clothes".

John: "I don't need to promise that, Martha, for your clothes wouldn't fit her anyway".

40. I DON'T THINK I'LL MARRY

Jane: "Any word of the big day, Sarah?".

Sarah: "Ah, I don't think I'll ever get married".

Jane: "What makes you say that, Sarah?".

Sarah: "When he is drunk, I don't want to marry him and when he is sober, he doesn't want to marry me".

41. BETTER IN THE MORNING

A woman who wasn't blessed with good looks had the misfortune of sharing a train compartment with a very drunk man.

Woman: "You disgust me; you are the worst looking man I have seen for a long time".

Drunk: "And you are the worst looking woman I have seen for a long time, but I'll look better in the morning".

42. IN THE ARMS OF ANOTHER

The young Minister asked his older Colleague for some tips on speaking at wedding receptions.

Old Minister: "Get a main thought in your mind and build around it". He added, "If the people are not showing much interest, startle them with the following comment. 'The happiest days of my life were spent in the arms of another man's wife.' That will catch their attention and then you can say, 'Yes, I spent them in the arms of my mother'".

The young Minister tried it out at his next wedding reception. He said, "I have a confession to make; The happiest days of my life were spent in the arms of another man's wife". He had a captive audience as they waited for him to continue. After a moment's ackward silence, he said, "I forget who she was".

43. YOUNG MOTH-ERS

John was very interested in the subject of moths and read many articles about them.

John: "Dad, I bought a book about moths and though I have read it from

cover to cover, it mentions nothing about moths".
Dad: "What is the title of the book?".
John: "Hints to young mothers". (He mistook it for Moth-ers).

44. BRINGING MOTHER HOME
Mary: "When you have a row with your husband, do you say you will go home to your mother?".
Jane: "No, I say I'll bring mother home".

45. DINNA KEN
An English man and his wife were touring Scotland and came across a big wedding. He stopped for some information.
Tourist: "Who is getting married today?".
Scotsman: "I dinna ken".
Later in the holiday they met a large funeral and, as they were waiting for it to pass, he inquired again.
Tourist: "Whose funeral is that?".
By-stander: "I dinna ken".
Tourist: "He didn't last long; did he?".

46. VALUABLE COW
The farmer's wife was ill, so he got a prescription from the doctor for her. His cow was also ill, so he got a prescription from the Vet for her. On taking the prescription to the Chemist, he said, "Don't mix them up, that's a valuable cow I've got".

47. FACE/BAKING POWDER
Mother to daughter: "Face powder might catch a man, but it is Baking powder that will keep him".

48. LOVE LETTERS
Betty: "Mammy, Susan and I found a big bunch of letters that Dad wrote to you before you married him. We decided to play Postman, so we put one through each letter box in the street, and believe it or not, there was the exact number for each house to get one".

49. I'M ALL COLD
John and Mary were duly married and went to live in Belfast.

She was from Ballymena, thirty miles away. They had twin beds.

Mary: "John, when my hands were cold in bed my mother always got me a pair of gloves.

John: "Then, I'll get your gloves for you".

Mary: "When my feet were cold in bed, mother always got me a water-bottle".

John: "Then I suppose I better get the water-bottle for you". Mary: When I was all cold, my mother always got into bed with me".

John (exasperated): "If you think that I'm going for your mother at this time of the night away to Ballymena, you are very much mistaken".

50. MARRIED THE POSTMAN
Tommy was posted overseas for a three year tour of service, but he promised to write every day to his girl friend. He faithfully kept his promise, but at the end of two years, she married the Postman.

51. A GOOD SWAP
Friend: "I see you have got a wee pup with you: where did you get it?".

Jack: "It is a pedigree pup and I got it for my wife".

Friend: "Knowing her, if you got it for your wife, you made a good swap".

52. DUST ON THE TABLE
The old bachelor married and was soon cross with his wife.

Husband: "Did you wipe the dust off the table?"

Wife: "Yes."

Husband: "Well, you did the wrong thing. I had a phone number written on it and now I can't contact the man. "

53. YOU WILL HAVE A MAN WHEN OTHERS HAVEN'T
Farmer's wife: "John, you lazy lump. It is dinner time and you are still in bed. Other women's husbands have been out working in the fields since early morning".

John: "Be thankful, for you will have a husband when the others haven't".

54. WILL I MARRY OR BUILD A GARAGE?
Bill: "I don't know what to do: whether to marry or build a garage".

Jim: "My advice is, play it safe and build a garage, for you can always back out of a garage".

55. BECAUSE OF YOUR MONEY YOU'RE HERE

The farmer was proudly showing his visitor around his farm.

Farmer: "Those hen houses hold 10,000 hens".

Wife chipped in: "And if it wasn't for my money they wouldn't be there".

Farmer to visitor: "Those two Silo sheds are a great boon. Most farmers have only one".

Wife: "And if it wasn't for my money you wouldn't even have one".

Farmer: "I'm proud of that tractor: it is the best one in the district".

Wife: "Yes, and if it wasn't for my money there would be no tractor".

Farmer (exasperated): "Be quiet woman. If it wasn't for your money, you wouldn't be here either".

56. HANDMAIDEN

Minister to prospective Bridegroom: "I hear you are about to take unto yourself a Handmaiden".

Bridegroom: "I don't know about being 'handmade', but she is well put together".

57. DOGGY BAG

At the wedding reception, the little girl had been given more meat than she could eat. The father, not wanting to see it wasted, asked the waiter if he could have a doggy bag.

Whereupon, the little girl said, "Oh, Daddy, are we going to get a dog?".

58. FATHER IN THE PRAM

The Young man went to a place in the interior of Africa and found everyone young. There wasn't an old person about the place. On making enquiries as to the reason, he was told that the witch doctor made pills which kept the population looking young. He purchased a supply and sent them home to his parents, instructing them to take one a day. Some years later he returned home unexpectedly and saw this young woman pushing a pram near his home. On seeing him, she exclaimed, "John, is it you? We didn't know you were home".

John: "Who are you, by the way? I don't recognise you".

Lady: "I'm your mother. I took some of those pills you sent us and they have kept me young".

John: "Where is my father?".

Lady: "That's him in the pram. He took an overdose of the pills " .

59. COLLECTION PLATE

The guest in the Church looked surprised when, during the Wedding Service, the Collection plate was passed around.

Collector: "Yes, Madam, it is most unusual, but the father of the bride requested it".

60. CARROTS

The Wedding Guests were enjoying the meal, but two girls set aside their carrots.

Male Guest: "Eat up your carrots, girls; they will make you look beautiful".

Girl: "They didn't do you much good, did they?".

61. MARRY RICH OR POOR GIRL

John: "I'm in a bit of a dilemma as to which girl I should marry: the poor girl I love, or the rich girl I don't think I love".

Harry: "My advice is....marry the one you love. By the way, maybe you will give me the address of the other one".

62. V.I.P. TREATMENT

The wife went to the marriage Counsellor for advice.

Wife: "My husband comes home drunk and I get so angry with him that I throw things at him and shout until I'm hoarse, but it makes no difference. What else can I do?"

Counsellor: "Try treating him nice for a change and see what happens".

The husband came home again drunk, but his wife tried to give him V.I.P. treatment. His coat was taken off and hung up and his slippers were put on his feet. He was placed in a cosy chair and given a kiss on the cheek.

His Reaction: "I don't know where I am, but I may as well enjoy it. The wife will beat me up anyway when I get home".

63. IS SHE DANGEROUS

Tom: "How is your wife? I hear she is quite ill. Is she dangerous?".

Billy: "No, she is too weak to be dangerous".

64. FOR BETTER OR FOR WORSE

Andy and his wife were having a row.

Wife: "Well, you took me for better or for worse".

Andy: "I know that, but you are worse than I took you for".

65. BIT OF FLUFF

The little rabbit was playing on the railway line when the points closed and nipped off his little tail. He ran home crying to Mammy rabbit. She sent him right back to look for it.

He spied it lying between the rails just where he had lost it. He put his head down to pick it up, but just then the points closed again...this time on his little head.

The moral of this story is...Don't loose your head over a little bit of fluff.

66. SUMMER IN MY HEART

The couple were celebrating their 50th wedding anniversary in the Hotel where they spent their Honeymoon. Getting ready to return home, the husband told his wife to hurry up or they would miss the last train home. They did miss it and had to return to the Hotel for another night.

Wife: "I may have Winter in my hair, but I have summer in my heart".

Husband: "If you had Spring in your feet, we wouldn't have missed the train".

67. THE ROOST

Boy: "Father calls our house 'the Roost'".

Friend: "Why".

Boy: "He says he is always henpecked".

68. SETTLE UP

The Wedding was over. The Bride's father got up and said to the guests "The happy couple will leave to settle down, while my wife and I will leave to settle up".

69. GUESTS TOASTED

Tom: "Why did the cannibal go to the wedding?".

Jim: "Because he heard they would be toasting a couple there".

70. PIE....MAKE IT HOT

The husband was henpecked and his wife had placed a cold pie in front of him for lunch.

Husband: "I'm not a complaining man, but if I did complain about this cold pie, what would you do?".

Wife: "I would make it hot for you".

71. SCUNNER
An appointment was made for the not-so-young couple to meet the Minister to discuss the wedding. The Minister waited a long time then the man arrived.
Man: "It is all off. I've taken a scunner at her".
Later, they patched up their difference and again an appointment was made with the Minister. After a long wait, the woman arrived alone.
Woman: "It is all off. I've taken a scunner at him".
Again they made up their differences and both made their way to the Manse. When the Minister saw them coming, he looked out the window and called out, "It's all off. I've taken a scunner at the both of you".

72. THIMBLE
Wife: "Look at you. There you are trying to sew a button on your shirt and the thimble is on the wrong finger".
Husband: "Yes, I know it is on the wrong finger. It should be on yours".

73. ASKED TO MARRY
Jane: "I have been asked to marry many times."
Mary: "Who asked you?".
Jane: "My father".

74. SMOTHER
The lady speaker waxed eloquently as she addressed the Mothers' Union on 'How to treat your husband', but she seemed to be getting nowhere.
Speaker: "Now ladies, hands up those who would like to mother their husbands". Only one hand went up.
Speaker: "I am surprised that there is only one lady among you who would like to mother her husband".
Woman: "I beg your pardon, Madam. I thought you said 'smother him'".

75. THRUST ON ME
The Bridegroom tried to get out of making a speech at the reception. When called upon to do so, he rose to his feet, put his hand on the Bride's shoulder and said, "This thing was thrust upon me". He wondered why everybody laughed.

76. MINISTER LATE FOR WEDDING

Years after the wedding the Minister met the former Bridegroom. The Minister had been late that day and kept everyone waiting.

Minister: "That was some fright I gave you that day."

Bridegroom: "Yes, and I've still got her."

77. BABY 9lbs

The neighbour called to see the new baby and Tommy overheard his mother tell her that the baby brother was nine pounds (in weight of course). Tommy was heard to complain, saying, "And to think a few more pounds would have got me a bike."

78. KARATE BLACK BELT

Tom: "Did you say your wife has a black belt in cookery?"

Fred: "Yes, that's right. She could kill a man with one chop."

79. NOTHING BURNED

Husband: "I'm home dear, you can serve the salad."

Wife: "How do you know we are having salad for tea.?"

Husband: "Because I couldn't smell anything burning when I came in."

80. COMMENT AFTER WEDDING

I think they will be very happy, for both of them are easily pleased!

81. MODEL HOME

Estate Agent: "Would you like to see a Model Home?"

Client: "I certainly would. What time does she stop work?"

82. BROKEN ENGAGEMENT

Friend: "Why did she break off the engagement?"

Young Man: "Unfortunately, I told her about my rich bachelor Uncle. Now she is my Aunt!"

83. KISSING GIRL GOODNIGHT

The young man had left his girlfriend home and was kissing her goodnight on the doorstep when her father opened the door.

Angry Father to young man: "I'll teach you to kiss my daughter."

Young Man: "I wish you could for she's not much good at it."

84. MARRIAGE LICENCE
Man to Minister who married them: "Are you sure you gave me a Marriage Licence?" I've had a dog's life ever since."

85. WONDER BOY
Neighbour: "Why do you call your husband 'Wonder Boy'?"
Woman; "Because every time I think of him I wonder."

86. IS THAT MULE A RELATIVE?
The honeymoon couple were having an argument and there was a long silence. After seeing a mule in a nearby field, the husband said, "Is that a relative of yours." The Bride of one week replied, "Yes, it's a relative of mine by marriage."

87. NOW WILL YOU GO TO CHURCH
The Minister was passing the house of one of his parishioners when he heard the man and wife shouting at each other. In fact he thought he heard a blow being struck. So, he opened the door and went in. There, to his horror, he saw the man hit his wife. When the man looked round and saw the Minister in the room, he shouted to his wife for the Minister to hear, "Now will you go to Church?"

88. I'LL LET YOU KNOW
On a T.V. programme a man and his wife were being questioned separately. The interviewer asked the wife: "When did your husband last tell you he loved you?"
Wife: "On the 15th of August six years ago."
The husband was called in and he was asked, "When did you last tell your wife that you loved her."
Husband: "On the 15th of August six years ago."
Interviewer: "That's remarkable. Both you and your wife gave the same answer. How can you remember what you did all those years ago?"
Husband: "Well, we were married on the 15th August six years ago. That night I told my wife I loved her and told her that if I changed my mind I would let her know."

AFTER HOSPITALITY

31. CONTESTED WILL
A lady died and left £8,000 in her Will to be divided equally between her cat and her dog.
Lawyer: "I think there is going to be trouble over the terms of the Will. I understand the Budgie is going to contest it".

Application: I can assure the ladies that there is no disagreement regarding the Supper to us this Evening. Of course, the Ladies of this congregation are noted for their excellent hospitality. Thanks.

32. LEAVE THE ROOM?
The boy and his sisters were invited out to a friend's house for a meal. They had always been taught to say "May I leave the table?" before getting up from it.
Boy: Smith, may I leave the table?".
Smith: "Yes, you may. It is about the only thing you have left".

Application: Were it not for the abundance of food provided tonight, we, too, would have left nothing but the table. Yes, as we look around, despite our big appetites, there is enough left to feed us all again. Thanks, etc.

33. FOUR WIVES MEET
(This is most suitable when the function is in the country).
Four school girl chums met after a long period of time and were anxious to get caught up on each other's news. The talk soon came round to husbands and the conversation went as follows:
First Lady: "My husband is a tailor and he keeps me well dressed for nothing".
Second Lady: "My husband is a Doctor and he keeps me well for nothing".
Third Lady: My husband is a Minister and he makes me good for nothing".
Fourth Lady: "My husband is a farmer and he makes me work for nothing".

Application: Whatever your husband works at, it has made no difference to the wonderful baking and preparation that has gone into providing the Supper this Evening. We may offer you nothing in return, but I trust your reward will be found in the knowledge that we have eaten so much and left so little. Thanks.

34. COLLECTION/OFFERING

The family were having dinner when Mummy noticed young John giving Fido, the dog, a good portion of his chicken. She checked him and said, "John, you musn't give the dog your chicken".
After dinner, John gathered up what was left on the plates and gave it to Fido, saying, "I'm sorry, Fido, I am not allowed to give you an offering, but here is the Collection".

Application: Fido may have got the Collection but we got the real offering. There were no left-overs for us and the sandwiches, cakes and pastry which we all enjoyed represent many hours of dedicated baking. We are most fortunate to have been here tonight. I, accordingly thank the ladies on behalf of all here tonight.

35. DELICIOUS

A Jewish Rabbi and a Roman Catholic Priest were travelling together on a train and, when lunch time came, they decided to share their sandwiches.
Rabbi: "What kind of meat is in your sandwiches?".
Priest: " I have pork in mine".
Rabbi: " I ' m sorry, but I can't. My religion doesn't allow me to eat pork".
Priest: "There is no one in the compartment but the two of us: try one, they are delicious".
Rabbi: "Indeed, it tastes nice. Did your wife make them?"
Priest: "No, my religion doesn't allow me to have a wife".
Rabbi: "You should try one: they are delicious".

Application: Where would we be without our wives? Many hours were spent by the ladies in the kitchen baking and preparing sandwiches. If it had been left to the men we would have to be satisfied with dry biscuits. Ladies, thank you most sincerely for this lovely Supper which you gave us. It, like yourselves, was delicious. We will recommend your baking to all and sundry.

36. CANNIBAL ILL
Explorer: "I hear the cannibal chief is ill".
Native: "Yes, the man he had for dinner yesterday didn't agree with him".

Application: There is no danger of anything we have partaken of this evening not agreeing with us. Everything was so appetising and so delicious and so efficiently served. We can do without some people, but we can't do without the Ladies . Thanks, etc.

37. MAKE A SPEECH
When Nero threw Christians to the lions, the arena was always packed with excited spectators. When the order was given, the gates were opened and a lion sprang into the arena and ran towards the solitary figure, hoping it would have a good meal.

As the lion stopped to weigh up the situation, the man whispered something to it, and the lion immediately turned tail and left the arena.

Another lion came out and the process was repeated. When Nero saw a third lion retreat he called to the man and said, "Tell me what you said to those lions and I'll spare your life".
Man: "All I said to each lion was 'If you eat me you will have to make a speech'".

Application: Well, that lot has fallen to me. The lion was able to refuse, but when I saw all the lovely things the ladies had prepared for us and then enjoyed them, I hadn't the will-power to refuse.

On behalf of all who partook of this lovely Supper, I would like to thank the Ladies most sincerely.

38. GREAT DANE
A man ran into a public house and said, "Who owns a black Poodle? It has just killed my Great Dane".
Man: "I own the black poodle, but how could it kill your Great Dane?".
Other man: "My Great Dane tried to eat it and it choked".

Application: I noticed that nobody here tonight choked. That would have been impossible for all those delicious items served to us just seemed to slide down. We kept on eating and the food kept disappearing. The only complaint we have is that we ate too much, but then, who could refuse such excellent baking? Thanks, etc.

39. DON'T SELL THE GOAT
Pat's mother was in hospital and time and time again she asked him to bring her some of her goat's milk. Just to make it taste more palatable, Pat began to put a drop of whiskey into the milk, but didn't mention this to his mother.

She relished the milk drink, but never made any comment. One night, as she felt the end was near, she called Pat over and whispered into his ear, "Pat, take your old mother's advice and don't sell that goat".

Application: We have had an excellent Supper, so efficiently served by the Ladies. One thing we are all agreed upon is that we needed nothing added to it to make it outstanding. It came to us straight from the kitchens...we partook of it with great relish. We thank the Ladies for such a good supper, and we also congratulate them on the high standard of their baking.

40. FISH MENU
The lodger was getting tired of the daily Menu. Every teatime he was served fish. He didn't object to having fish, but he didn't want it every day. One evening as the lady was setting the table, a fork fell to the floor.
Landlady: "That is a sign that a visitor is coming".
Lodger: "Well, I hope it is the butcher".

Application: It must be an awful thing not to be satisfied. The ladies have seen to our tastes and desires this evening. Watching those around me, I noticed that they refused nothing. It looked as if they were never going to stop. That, of course, is due to the good baking and efficient service of the ladies and on behalf of all present, I would say a big "Thank you" to them.

41. FARMER'S OWN FIELD
The farmer was awarded the trophy for being outstanding in his own field.

Application: I don't know about the Farmer, but I do know that the ladies who provided this lovely supper are outstanding in their own field....that is, the field of Baking. I'm sorry we haven't a trophy to present to you: you will have to be content with empty plates. Thanks, etc.

42. HARDLY WORTHWHILE GOING HOME

The visiting Minister arrived early for the morning Service, so he took a walk around the little graveyard. He met an old man and commented on the neatness of the place and asked whose grave he was attending to.

Man: "This is our family plot. My grandfather and my father are buried here. If God spares me, I'll be buried here, too".

Minister: "How old was your grandfather when he died?".

Man: "My grandfather was 85 when he died".

Minister: "How old was your father when he died?".

Man: "My father was also 85 when he died".

Minister: "And how old are you?".

Man: "I'm 84 and 10 months".

Minister: "In that case, it is hardly worth your while going home".

Application: Well, the way I and my colleagues feel, it is hardly worth our while going home. We are full up after this lovely Supper. Thanks to the ladies, etc.

43. SAUSAGES GUTTED

The lodger was being served fish and salads so often that he longed for something from the butchers. One day he brought home a pound of sausages.

Lodger: "I would like you to fry some of these for my tea".

Landlady: "I've never cooked sausages...what do I do with them?".

Lodger: "Just fry them the way you fry the fish".

Landlady (putting shrivelled things on the plate): "There's not much in them once you gut them".

Application: We smile, but we are also very pleased that those who prepared the Supper this evening are experts in culinary matters. There was nothing we could refuse, consequently, the plates were emptied as quickly as they were filled. We thank the Ladies for adding tremendously to the success of the evening.

44. LOST 40 LBS.

Mary: "I've lost 40 lbs. Aren't you going to congratulate me?".

Jane: "I can't believe it, you look much the same to me".

Mary: "Well, it's true...I've lost 5 lbs. eight times".

Application: If we are weight-watchers, we shouldn't be here this evening. Try as we would, we couldn't resist the lovely things served to us this Evening. Rather than losing a few pounds, we have all added to our weight. We thank the ladies for this excellent Supper.

45. LIKE NECTAR

The man and his wife had travelled far and long and they were tired, thirsty and hungry. They stopped at a Service Restaurant and ordered a pot of tea to start with.

Lady: "This tea tastes like nectar to me".

Waitress: "Don't blame me. If you have any complaints, make them to the manager".

Application: There will be no complaints about the Supper tonight. It has surpassed all our expectations. We were ready for it and, judging by the little that is left, we did it justice. We came in empty and we are going out full. Thanks, etc.

46. OPENED A TIN OF PEAS

The new neighbour had just arrived and she and the lady next door got chatting.

Lady: "This time last year I lost my husband".

New neighbour: "I'm sorry to hear that. What happened to him?".

Lady: "I was preparing the dinner and I said to him, 'John, take this sharp knife and go down the garden and cut me a cabbage'. On his was down the garden, he tripped and fell right on the knife. It pierced his heart and he died".

New neighbour: "That was awful, what did you do?".

Lady: "I had to open a tin of peas".

Application: There were no calamities or emergencies tonight. Everything went according to plan as far as the Supper was concerned. I can assure the Ladies that it was a great success. Perhaps when you saw us devour the sandwiches and cakes, you thought there wouldn't be enough to feed us all and that you would have to open a tin of biscuits. You need not have worried, for there was more than enough even though we did our best to leave nothing. That speaks for itself. Thanks, etc.

47. RHUBARB TART

The newly-wed husband expressed a wish that his new Bride would bake him a Rhubarb Tart. Anxious to please, she made the effort even though she hadn't baked one before. Evening came and she proudly set the Rhubarb Tart before him.

Husband: "What sort of an appetite do you think I have? That Rhubarb Tart is at least two feet long".

Wife: "I know, but I looked everywhere and those were the shortest stalks I could find".

Application: Tonight everything the ladies served was just right. It would have been impossible to find fault with any item put before us. The sandwiches and cakes were just perfect and so appetising. In fact, the way we attacked them must have shown you that we were in our element. Thanks, etc.

48. HUNGRY GORBS

One of my Ministerial colleagues was telling me that he visited a farm where one of his members lived. She offered him a cup of tea and something to eat. While eating, he noticed a cat come to the door which the lady soon chased away.

Minister: "Do you get many cats coming to your door?".

Woman: "Hold your tongue: all the hungry gorbs come here".

Application: The woman opened her mouth and put her foot in it. She didn't mean to imply that the Minister was one of the "Hungry gorbs ".

Nevertheless, we could forgive you if you concluded that all the hungry gorbs had gathered here this evening. We couldn't help gorging ourselves and we apologise if we have left you nothing to take home. You have only yourselves to blame for giving us such a lovely Supper. Thanks.

49. LONG LANE

The visitor to a country cousin arrived at the door a bit exhausted and commented: "That is a very long land you have".

Lady: "Yes, it is a long lane, but if it was any shorter it wouldn't reach".

Application: Some of us have come a short distance tonight and a number of us have come a long way to get here. are we complaining? By no means.

The lovely supper we enjoyed this evening leaves it impossible for us to complain. Those who missed it will be sorry when we tell them how well we were treated.

We may have come to your door empty, but I can assure you we are going away full. Some half-cousins met for a meal and, as they were leaving, one of them commented, "We were half-cousins when we started the meal; now we are full cousins". That is how we feel tonight. Thanks, etc.

50. HITCH HIKER
The lorry Driver gave a hitch-hiker a lift of 100 miles. The man insisted on paying the driver, but the driver said 'No' for he was glad of the company. As he left the lorry, the hitch-hiker reached over and pushed something into the driver's breast pocket, saying, "That will get you something to drink".

The lorry driver thought nothing more about it until he was getting ready for bed.
Driver to wife: "Have a look in my coat pocket and see how much that fellow left me for a drink".
Wife: "You won't believe this, but he left you two tea bags".

Application: It is putting it mildly to say he was disappointed. We came here tonight with high expectations, knowing the reputation the ladies here have for making excellent Suppers. We were not disappointed. We came in empty and thanks to the ladies, we are going out full.

51. GREYHOUND
The fat boy had been spending part of his school holidays at his Granny's house .
Granny: "Tom, you are eating too much. By the end of the week I'll have you looking like a prize greyhound" .
Later, he was out walking and met a greyhound in the street.
Tom to greyhound: "By the look of you, you have been visiting your granny's, too".

Application : Unlike this boy, tonight's Supper has brought us all closer together in that we have put on a couple of inches to our waistline . If you want to slim, this is not the place for you . Thanks, etc.

52 . CAN CHEW, BUT CAN'T SWALLOW

The Sunday School party was in full swing and eats were being served .
Lady: "Come on, son, have something else to eat".
Boy: "I couldn't. I've got to the stage where I can chew, but can't swallow".

Application: If we were honest, we would admit being like that boy. It may have been our intention to eat in moderation, but the Supper was so delicious that we couldn't hold back .
We, too, about reached the stage where we could chew, but couldn't swallow. Thanks, etc.

53. GRACE AT MEALS

In the class for Religious Instruction, the teacher was trying to impress upon her class the meaning of Grace before meals.
Teacher: "Tommy, what does your father say before you begin your meal?"
Tommy: "Please, Miss, he says 'Go easy on the butter for it is dear these days'".

Application: We didn't hear anyone telling us to go easy. Rather we were told to eat up and, with everything so appetising and so efficiently served, we couldn't do otherwise than comply . Thanks, etc.

54. SEA WATER SOLD OUT

The old lady was visiting the seaside for the very first time. A friend asked her to bring back a bottle of sea water for her to bathe her feet in. Upon arriving at the Coastal town she walked up to an old fisherman who was relaxing, and innocently asked him, "How much is your sea-water a bottle?". Not wishing to lose an opportunity of making a few pence, he replied, "10p per bottle". She bought a bottle full!

Later in the afternoon, she met the same man at the same place and, noting that the tide was out, she said, "I'm glad I bought the water early, for I see you are nearly sold out".

Application: We have enjoyed a lovely supper this evening and we had all we could eat. At no time was there any danger of being 'sold out', or running short of eats. Your hospitality has brought this evening to a very enjoyable close and it only remains for me, on behalf of all present, to thank the ladies for such a generous supper.

MISCELLANEOUS STORIES

51. STICK STAMPS
The old lady went into the Post office and asked for three stamps and got them.
Lady: "Must I stick them on myself?".
Assistant: "No, stick them on the envelopes".

52. GROCERIES IN POST OFFICE
The old country lady went into a city Post office and asked for three stamps, half a dozen eggs and 1lb of butter.
Clerk: "We don't sell eggs or butter".
Woman: "Shame on you in a Post Office this size. Our wee Post Office sells eggs and butter as well as stamps".

53. TIRED QUICKLY
Employer: "John, you talk slowly, you walk slowly and you work slowly. Is there anything you can do quickly?".
John: "Yes, I tire quickly".

54. MOTHER'S BIRTHDAY
It was mother's birthday and her daughter baked a cake for the occasion.
Mother: "Why are there only five candles on the cake?".
Daughter: "We thought you would rather remember the size of your shoes than the years of your age".

55. CARETAKER COULDN'T WRITE
A German Jew fled to England during the war and sought help from fellow Jews. They offered him a job as Caretaker in the local Synagogue. Among his duties he would have to write out a weekly report stating the number of hours the light was burned and how many evenings the premises were used, etc.
Jew: "I am very sorry, but I can't take the job for I can neither read nor

write".

He eventually went to America, opened a chain of grocery stores and became a Millionaire. One day he went into his bank to withdraw a considerable sum of money. The Bank manager was new to the area and asked the Jew to sign his name.

Jew: "I sign with an X, for I can neither read nor write".

Bank Manager: "I find that most incredible. A Millionaire and you can neither read nor write! What would you have been if you could read and write?".

Jew: "To tell you the truth, I would have been a Caretaker in a Liverpool Synagogue".

56. APPLIED ELECTRICITY

The client in America engaged a Lawyer to trace his "family tree". After some time, the lawyer contacted him.

Lawyer: "We have come up against a problem. I find that one of your ancestors committed murder and died in the electric chair".

Client: "If that is so, just forget about the whole thing".

Lawyer: "No, we can't leave it; just leave it to me and I will think up something".

When the final report came to hand, the client quickly looked to see whether the relation of disrepute was included. He was and against his name was written, "He occupied the Chair of Applied Electricity in a Public Institution".

The Lawyer was duly paid by a grateful client.

57. CALL IT A DAY

The woman had six boys and was expecting another child.

 Friend: "What will you call the new baby?".

Woman: "If it is a girl we will call it Adele".

Friend: "And if it is a boy what will you call it?".

Woman: "If it is a boy, we will call it 'A Day'".

58. DON'T WANT TO GO TO SCHOOL

The man was very conscious of the passing years and was unduly worried about growing older. When he was offered some pills which would rejuvenate him and make him feel younger, he quickly bought them. In his zeal, he took a large dose before going to bed.

Wife, next morning: "John, it is time to get up".
John: "Let me lie on: I don't want to go to school today".

59. APPLE .... SMALL PIECE

Tom was given an apple by his mother to divide between him and his little sister.
Sister: "Look, you gave me the small piece and you kept the big piece for yourself . That's not fair" .
Tom: "What would you have done if you had cut the apple?".
Sister: "I would have kept the small piece and given you the bigger bit".
Tom: "Well, what are you crying for? Haven't you got the small piece? ".

60. LAYING PAVEMENTS

Friend: "What are all your hens doing in your front garden this morning?"
.Neighbour: "They heard some man say they were going to lay a pavement and they want to see how it is done".

61. OAT CAKE

The Tramp called at the house and asked the lady for a piece of bread. She gave him an oat cake with some jam on it. The tramp licked the jam off it and returned the oat cake, saying, "Your jam was nice, Missus, here is your wee board back".

62. THINGS THAT CONTAIN MILK

Teacher: "Billy, name five things that contain milk". Billy, hesitantly, "Butter, cheese, ice cream and two cows".

63. BUY A GOLD FISH

Customer: "I don't like the look of this cod fish".
Waiter: "Madam, if it is looks you want, I suggest you buy a goldfish" .

64. GRASS LONGER AT BACK

The Tramp, looking for a meal, knocked at the front door of the house and then, to make an impression, he stepped on to the front lawn and started to eat the grass. He hoped to give the impression that he was desperately hungry.
Woman, opening door: "Poor man, you must be hungry: come round to the back garden where the grass is much longer".

65. ORGANIST

Boy: "My grandfather was a professional Organist, but he had to give it up".
Friend: "Why did he give it up?".
Boy: "He stopped playing the Organ after his monkey died".

66. GRANDFATHER CLOCK

The man was carrying a grandfather clock round to the Jewellers to have it fixed. Accidentally, he bumped into an elderly lady. In an angry voice, she said, "Why don't you be like other people and wear a wrist watch".

67. LUMBERJACK

The winner of the tree-felling competition was congratulated and was asked, "Where did you learn to cut down trees so fast?".
Lumberjack: "In the Sahara Desert".
Judge of competition: "But there are no trees in the Sahara Desert".
Lumberjack: "Not now, there aren't".

68. SCHOOL PRINCIPAL REQUIRED

The Post of School Principal was advertised and the Vice-Principal felt sure that he would be appointed. He was greatly disappointed when a much younger man got the Post.
Vice-Principal: "I don't think it is fair. I have had 25 years experience teaching P7".
Chairman of Board: "No, you don't have 25 years teaching experience. You have one year's experience 25 times. Now, do you understand why you didn't get the Principal-ship?".

69. BOILING EGGS

Housewife: "I don't use an egg-timer when boiling eggs".
Friend: "What do you use?".
Housewife: "I find 'Onward Christian soldiers' ideal for the job".
Friend: "How?".
Housewife: "I sing one verse for soft boiled eggs; two verses for medium boiled eggs, and three verses for hard boiled eggs".

70. POTATO/ONION CROSSED

John: "What do you get when you cross a potato with an onion?".

Jim: "I don't know. What do you get when you cross a potato with an onion?".
John: "You get potatoes with watery eyes".

71. SHEEP/KANGAROO CROSSED

John: "What do you get when you cross a sheep with a Kangaroo?".
Jim: "I don't know. What do you get when you cross a sheep with a kangaroo?".
John: "You get woolly jumpers".

72. HOW IS JACK RABBIT?

First Rabbit: "How is Jack Rabbit? Do you ever hear from him?".
Second Rabbit: "Yes, I had a litter from him last week".

73. OSTRICH EGG

The wee boy bought a bantam hen and each morning he kept looking for an egg. When the hen eventually laid an egg, he was disappointed with the size of it. There was an ostrich egg hanging up in the house, so he took it to the hen and, putting it in front of the hen, said, "Now, I want you to keep your eye on that egg and do your very best.

74. RIGHT MAN HOME?

The deceased was brought home in his coffin and the funeral service commenced. The Minister extolled at great length the virtues of the deceased and eulogised him in an exaggerated way.
The widow became restless, then turned to her daughter and said, "Go and have a look in the coffin and see if they brought the right man home".

75. WIFE FELL OUT

The Pilot of the little single engine plane was giving rides at £5 a time.
Scotsman: "That's too expensive; I wouldn't pay that".
Pilot: "I'll make a deal with you. I'll take you and your wife up. If you don't call out or shout, I'll not charge you anything. Of course, if you do call out or shout, then you pay up".
Scotsman: "I agree".
The Pilot, who was a mischievous fellow, did everything he could to scare the Scotsman. He somersaulted over and over again. He looped the loop, but not a sound came from the Scotsman.

Pilot (on ground): "Well, you earned your free ride. I felt sure you would yell out when I did some of those manoeuvres".
Scotsman: "To tell you the truth, I nearly did shout out when the wife fell out of the plane".

76. HIT HIM AGAIN

The Chairman tried again and again to get the speaker to stop talking and sit down. In exasperation he lifted his mallet in order to hit the table. As he did so, he hit the head of a man who was dozing beside him. As he began to apologise to the man, the man said, "Never mind, hit me again; I can still hear him".

77. NIAGARA FALLS

The Canadian was showing the American some of the famous places in Canada, but the American ridiculed them all and spoke of greater things in America. Eventually, they came to Niagara Falls.
Canadian: "Well, what do you think of our famous Horse-shoe Falls? Millions of visitors come every year to see them?".
American: "To us, that is only a leak, but I know a plumber in Texas who could repair that leak in a few hours".

78. WHERE'S YOUR GRAMMAR?

Salesman: "Is your mother in?".
Boy: "No, she ain't never in at this time".
Salesman: "Boy, where is your grammar?".
Boy: "She is in bed; she always lies down in the afternoon".

79. MADE IN POLAND

A friend of mine bought a "Potty" in Woolworth's for her baby. When she got home, she was amused to see a label on the bottom which read, "Made in Poland".

80. FRAMES £1 NOTE

A friend noticed a £1 note neatly framed and hanging on the wall.
Friend: "What is the significance of the framed one pound note?".
Lady: "That was the first £1 note my husband earned. Incidentally, the frame cost two shillings (10p). Now the frame is worth one pound and the pound is worth two shillings".

43

81. I'M THE LIGHTHOUSE
The ship's captain saw a light ahead of him. He signalled, "Move ten degrees to the North".
The reply came back, "You move ten degrees to the south".
He signalled again, "I'm captain....move ten degrees to the North".
The reply came back: "I'm a Seaman, first class. Move ten degrees to the South".
He signalled again, "I'm a Battleship...move as I say, ten degrees to the North".
The reply came: "I'm a Lighthouse....move ten degrees South".

82. MEAN FELLOW
He took his girl friend to Portrush
Fellow: "There is some nice chocolate; you should buy yourself a bar".
She told her mother when she got home.
Mother: "You mean you had to pay for it yourself?".
Girl; "Yes, mother".
Mother: "Did he pay for your train fare?".
 Girl: "Yes, he did".
Mother: "Then take it right back to the mean fellow".
Girl to fellow: "Here is the money for the train fare you bought for me".
Fellow: "There was no hurry; it would have been time enough at the week-end".

83. RED CURRANTS
He decided to grow tomatoes for the show. He won first prize for red currants.

84. QUACK QUACK
Some ducks were crossing the road in Ballymena.
First duck: "Quack, Quack".
Second Duck: "I cannae go any quacker".

85. GLASS OF WATER IN BARBER'S
The Barber had cut Pat's face so much when shaving him:
Pat: "Can you let me have a glass of water, please?".
Barber: "Are you going to faint?".
Pat: "No, I just want to see if my mouth can still hold water".

86. PINCH HER SEAT

Two women were travelling home on the Bus. As they drove through a rough quarter of the City, two men got on the Bus and stood close to where the women were sitting.

First woman: "As you stand up to get off, don't turn just walk out backwards. I'll tell you why when we get out".

Second woman: "Why had we to walk out backwards".

First woman: "I distinctly heard one of those men say to the other that as soon as we got up, they would pinch our seats".

87. PARROT CAN COUNT

Parrot to coal man: "Throw in ten bags of coal".

Coalman: "I've left ten bags in: you are a very clever parrot".

Parrot: "I can count, too, you only left nine bags in. Bring the tenth one".

88. MISSED OPPORTUNITY

The man spoke at a gathering and, afterwards, asked his wife what she thought of his effort.

Wife: "You missed two opportunities half way through".

Husband: "What were they?".

Wife: "The first one was to shut up and the other one was to sit down".

89. CONNOISSEUR OF WINES

The Connoisseur of Wines challenged the audience to test his ability to taste and name any wine even though blind-folded.

When blind-folded, they set out a variety of wines, plus one glass of water. To the amazement of all, he was able to correctly name each wine just by tasting it. At last he came to the glass of water. He sipped it once; then twice, and after the third attempt, he said, "You have me beaten here. I can't name it, but I can tell you this....it won't sell!".

90. LIGHT OF MY LIFE IS GONE OUT

The man's wife died and he had the Inscription "The Light of my life has gone out" put on the headstone.

Later, he married again and instructed the Sculptor to add, "But I have struck another match".

91. WHERE'S THE FIRE?

The dear old lady had a fear of fires and when she stayed in a Hotel, one of the first things she did was find out where the Fire Escape was positioned. The Clerk at the desk told her to go along the corridor, turn right, then left, and the first door leads to the Fire Escape. She got mixed up and took the wrong turning. On opening the door in front of her she was confronted by a man in the bath. "Oh", she exclaimed, "I'm looking for the Fire Escape". As she hurriedly retreated, the man came running after her with a towel tied around him, shouting, "Where's the fire? Where's the fire?".

92. TONGUE FOR TEA

Lady: "Would you like a bit of tongue for tea?".
Visitor: "No thanks, I would never eat anything out of an animal's mouth".
Lady: "Is there anything else you would like?".
Visitor: "I'll just have a boiled egg".

93. BOWLER'S SKIP

A member of the Bowling Club died. Two other members tried to contact him through a Spiritualist Medium. When contact was made, the following conversation took place.
Member: "Do you do any bowling where you are?".
Deceased: "Yes, we do a lot of bowling".
Member: "What are the bowling greens like?".
Deceased: "Better than any I have ever played on".
Member: "Do you play any competitions?".
Deceased: "Yes, we do. We have a big one next week and I see your name is down to act as Skip".

94. PULLOVER?

The dear old lady was driving her car. There was nothing unusual in that, but a Speed Cop noticed that while she drove, she was also knitting. He decided to reprimand her. He caught up with her and shouted, "Pullover".
She smiled and replied, "No, it is a pair of socks for my old man".

95. DOG RUNNING AFTER BICYCLE

A lady wrote to the "Agony Aunt" in a Magazine, saying that her dog runs after people on a bicycle. "What should she do?", she asked.
The Agony Aunt replied, "My advice is: take the bicycle from it".

96. SLIPPED ONE FORWARD....TWO BACK

The boy arrived late for school on a frosty morning and the teacher asked for an explanation.

Boy: "The road was so slippery every time I took a step forward, I slipped back two".

Teacher: "If that was so, how did you get to school at all?".

Boy: "I turned around and started to walk backwards".

97. COFFIN HIT THE TREE

The quarrelsome wife had died and as her coffin was being carried down the country lane, it touched the over-hanging branch of a tree. To the Undertaker's astonishment, he heard a movement within the coffin. The knock had revived the corpse. They returned to the house and the woman lived for another six months and then died. As the coffin was being carried down the lane, the husband of the woman spoke up and said, "Be careful of that tree when you are passing it".

98. THREE MINUTES TO LIVE

Prison Warder to condemned man: "Well, Mate, your time has come and you have only about three minutes to live".

Prisoner: "Is there nothing you can do for me?".

Warder: "I could boil you an egg".

99. SAREE....SARONG

Man to Indian Lady: "That is a very nice Saree you are wearing".

Lady: "It is not a Saree....it is a sarong".

Man: "Oh, I'm saree I was sarong".

100. SIZE 6 $^{7/8}$

The American Negro joined the Army and was asked what his name was.

Man: "My name is 6 $^{7/8th}$ Smith".

Sergeant: "Don't try to make a fool of me. That's no name".

Man: "Well it is my name. When I was born all my relatives wanted me to be named after them. My father solved the problem by putting all their names in his hat, saying that the first one out would be given to me. The first that came out of his hat was 6 $^{7/8}$ and that is what they called me".

101. FOUR THINGS RELATING TO OLD AGE

The Lecturer started by saying that there are four things that show that one is getting old. The first, he said, was hardness of hearing. The second was dimness of eye sight. The third was failing memory. The fourth, he said; then after a long pause he confessed, "I'm afraid I forget what the fourth thing is".

102. MADE WRONG

Wife to husband: "I think you were made wrong for as far as I can see it is your nose that runs and your feet that smell".

103. COMMERCIAL TRAVELLER'S EXPENSE ACCOUNT

Boss: "Your expense sheet is very high. What is that large amount for?".
Traveller: "That was for my hotel".
Boss: "Well, don't buy any more Hotels".

104. BEE IN COW'S EAR.

Farmer: "Did you hear about the Bee that flew into the cow's ear?"
Friend: "No, What happened to the Bee that flew into the cow's ear?"
Farmer: "It ended up in a pail of milk."
Friend: "How did that happen?"
Farmer: "It went in one ear and out the udder."

105. CROSS-EYED SERGEANT

The new recruits paraded in front of the cross-eyed Army Sergeant.
Sergeant to first man: "What is your name?".
Second man: "Billy Smith, Sir".
Sergeant: "I didn't speak to you".
Third man: "I didn't speak, Sir".

106. LADY GODIVA

Mary: "The drama committee met last night and unanimously agreed that you take the part of Lady Godiva in the play next month.
Jane: "I'm terribly sorry. I won't be able to do that, for I have something on that night".

107. THE ISRAELITE

The tenement building had burned down and people were being interviewed.

First man: "I think it was due to the electric light on the third floor".

Second man: "I think it was due to the gas light on the second floor".

Third man: "Actually, in my opinion, it was due to the Israelite on the first floor".

108. BANANA ON THE TRAIN

Two men who had never eaten a banana before bought some to eat on the train. As one of them began to eat his banana, the train entered a tunnel and everything went dark. He called out to the other man: "Don't eat that banana: I took a bite of mine and I have gone blind".

109. FREE TICKETS

The woman and her young son asked for tickets on British Airways.

Official: "How old is your son?".

Woman: "He is three years old".

The official was sceptical and so he said to the boy, "How old are you?".

Boy: "I'm three".

Official: "Tell me, what happens to little boys who tell lies?".

Boy: "They travel free on British Airways".

110. BOY AND BAG

The troublesome boy was sent to a Camp in the hope that his behaviour would improve. When asked later how he got on at Camp, he said he had learned to swim. He said he went down the river for about two miles. "Great", said his friend. "Had you any difficulty?". The boy replied: "My biggest difficulty was getting out of the bag"

111. PLATE WITH SHIP

The landlady set a plate down before the lodger which had a ship painted on it, but what she put on the plate was rather skimpy. . . . just one potato, one vegetable and a wee bit of meat. When she asked the lodger what he thought of it, he replied, "There's no danger of the cargo sinking the ship".

112. BAD WORDS

The teacher chastised a boy in school for using a 'bad word'.

Teacher: "Where did you hear that word?".

Boy: "I heard it from my father".

Teacher: "Well, don't ever use it again. You don't even know what it means".

Boy: "Yes, I know what it means. It means the car won't start".

113. ELEPHANT FOR SALE.

Advertisement in Dublin Newspaper: "Circus owner has Elephant for Sale. Bargain at £2,000. Please add £1,500 for Postage and Packing.

114. MUSEUM MUMMY

The attendant was showing a group of visitors around the Museum.

Guide: "This Mummy you are looking at is six thousand and five years old."

Visitor: "How can you date it so precisely ?

Guide: "That's easy. I have been here for five years and I was told it was six thousand years old when I started the job."

115. TEMPORARY JOB

A Foundry worker told of a time when the firm had to "lay off" a number of its employees. He recalled how a man aged 61 years had been with the firm since he was 14. When told that he was being made redundant, he said in all seriousness, "If I had known this was only a temporary job, I would never have taken it in the first place."

116. PAT HOME FROM SPAIN.

Pat went to Spain for a holiday and came back looking well with a great tan. Shortly after he got back home he had a heart attack and dropped dead. He was duly laid out for the wake and neighbours called to sympathise with the widow. Mrs. Murphy was one of those who called.

Mrs Murphy: "Doesn't he look great with that tan. He's a picture of health."

Wife: "Yes, the holiday in Spain did him a world of good."

Mrs. Murphy: "He looks so happy, too."

Wife : "Yes, he died in his sleep and he doesn't know he's dead yet."

Mrs. Murphy: " Oh, that's terrible. When he wakes up and finds himself dead , the shock will kill him."

117. ADVERT IN PAPER

"Wanted urgently, a large Budgie cage for an old age pensioner"

118. DOG ON ESCALATOR.
Pat read the notice: "Dogs must be carried on the Escalator."
He exclaimed, "Where am I to get a dog at this time of the evening?"

119. TWO IN THE DESERT.
Two Irishmen's plane came down in the Desert. As they crawled along the sand one asked the other, "What day is this ?"
The other replied, "It is the twelfth of July."
The other replied, " At least they are getting a good day for their walk back in Belfast. "

120. SAY FEES.
A photographer at a dinner for Lawyers came up with a unique way for getting them to smile for the Camera. He simply said, "Say fees."

121. FLY LIKE A BIRD.
A man tried to get a job in a stage show.
Producer: "What can you do?"
Man: "I imitate birds."
Producer: "I'm sorry, but I'm not interested. People who imitate birds can be had by the thousands and nobody will pay money to see them."
Man: "Well, it is evident you don't want me," he said, as he spread his arms and flew out the window.

122. NO STAMPS.
One day mother sent her little boy to post a letter and gave him the money to pay for the stamp. He was soon back, looking all pleased with himself.
"Mammy," he said, " I fooled the people at the Post Office. When no one was looking I dropped the letter into the box without any stamp. Here is your money back.

123. THIS IS WHERE YOUR HEART IS.
Teacher: "This is where your heart is," pointing to her chest.
Little boy: "Mine is where I sit down."
Teacher: " Whatever gave you that idea?"
Little boy: "Well, Miss, every time I do something good my grandma pats me right there and says, 'Bless your little heart.' "

124. PROTECTION FROM BURGLARS

A retired Policeman was reminiscing and told of an incident that happened when he and his colleague were on the beat. It was in a rural area and one evening they noticed a ladder against the wall of a house leading to a half open window. They felt it was their duty to alert the owner to the danger this could be. When they knocked, the old man opened the door.

Policeman: "Do you realise you are asking for trouble leaving a ladder there near an open window? Anyone could climb up the ladder and break into your home."

Old Man: "There's not much danger of that happening. The ladder is there to let the cat in and I took the precaution of sawing through some of the rungs half way up. Woe betide anyone who tries to climb up. He'll hit the ground before he knows it."

125. HALF THE COUNCIL ASLEEP!

The Reporter commented in the local newspaper that half the town council were asleep at the monthly meeting. The Chairman of the Council took grave exception to this and demanded an apology to be printed in the next edition. The Reporter obliged and stated that "Half the Council were not asleep."

126. HEAD UPSIDE DOWN

A bald man with a beard got on the bus and a small boy was overheard saying to his Mummy. "Look Mummy that man has got his head on upside down."

127. JOAN OF ARC

Teacher at History Lesson: "Who was Joan of Arc?"
Pupil: "Please miss, she was Noah's wife."

128. BURY ME WITH MY FLUTE

The Musician had given instructions that his flute should be buried with him. His wish was duly carried out. A friend remarked to his widow, "What did you think of your husband's request?" "Well," she replied, "I thought it was a blessing he didn't play the piano."

129. HI DONKEY

Two men were talking when a friend passed by.

Friend to one of them: "Hi, Donkey."
Companion: "Did you hear what he called you? He said, 'Hi, Donkey.' Why did he call you that?"
Man: "I don't know the reason but he haw, he hawlways calls me that."

130. SLEPT WITH DADDY
The little girl at school announced to her teacher, "Last night me slept with Daddy."
Wishing to correct her English, the Teacher said" "That is not correct. You should say, "I slept with Daddy last night"."
Little Girl: "That must have been after me went to sleep."

131. PHOTOGRAPHER'S SHOP
The following notice appeared in his window: "Some children can be very annoying at times when having their photo taken. We now have a special offer to parents. Children can be shot at home at no extra charge."

132. LEFT BEHIND
The man arrived out of breath at the Harbour.
Man: "Has the ferry left?"
Official: "The ferry is away, you are the one that's left."

133. DOMINOES
Man in Restaurant: "Will your band play anything I ask them to?"
Waiter: "Of course they are very versatile you know."
Man: "Ask them to play dominoes."

134. COPPER NITRATE
Science Teacher: Can anyone tell me what Copper Nitrate is?"
Pupil: "It is the payment a policeman receives when he works overtime."

135. SICK OF HIM
Tom: "Jimmy's mother said he lost his job because of sickness. Was it anything serious?"
John: "The Boss got sick of him, that's why."

136. APPLICANT FOR JOB
The cocky fellow walked into the Manager's office and asked if there was

an opening for him. The Manager replied, "Yes, there is one right behind you, and you can close it as you go out."

137. ORKNEYS
Father: "Why were you kept in at school today?"
Son: "Because I couldn't remember where the Orkneys are."
Father" "Well in future remember where you put them."

138. WE'LL SEND FOR YOU LATER
Having been examined by the Doctor at the Hospital the receptionist told the patient, "We will send for you in twelve months time." The Patient rather astonished at the long wait replied, "What good is that? I might be dead in twelve months!" The Receptionist always ready with an answer said, "Well if that is the case, your wife can let us know and we will cancel the appointment."

139. BED PAN
Nurse: "I'll bring you a pan in the morning."
Patient: "Do you mean I have to make my own breakfast?"

140. CONVALESCING
Hospital Visitor: "How is Mr Murphy?"
Nurse: "He is convalescing at the moment."
Visitor: "That's all right. I'll wait until he is finished."

141. TAKING MEDICINE
Man to passenger in bus: "My son is taking medicine at Queen's University."
Passenger: "I hope that it has helped him and that he is feeling better."

142. DROPPED ARCHES
Man: "My wife has dropped arches; can you suggest a cure?"
Doctor: "Yes, rubber heels."
Man: "What will I rub them with?"

🍀 IRISH STORIES 🍀

95. WHIST DRIVE
Husband: "Who was that at the door?".
Wife: "Somebody selling whist-drive tickets. I bought two".
Husband: "What was the point of that? Sure you know we can't play whist".
Wife: "I know we can't play whist, but I thought we would enjoy the drive".

96. HORSE AND CART ACCIDENT (another version of 49 in Vol.1)
The farmer was on his way home with his horse and cart when a lorry hit the cart and sent the farmer and his horse into the ditch. He saw some soldiers coming along and decided to lie still in the hope of claiming compensation. He kept thinking of what he would do with all the money he would get. An officer came along, looked at the horse and seeing it had broken a leg, he shot it. With his gun still in his hand he asked the farmer how he was. Seeing the gun and knowing what happened to the horse, the farmer quickly jumped up and said, "I never felt better".

97. WHAT TIME IS IT?
Barney: "What time is it, Pat?".
Pat: "It's not four o'clock yet".
Barney: "How do you know?".
Pat: "I told the wife I would be home by four o'clock, and I'm not home yet".

98. HAIRDRESSER'S ADVERTISEMENT
A sign in a Dublin Hairdresser's window read: "No appointment necessary. Hair cut while you wait".

99. 17.4 DEAD
Lecturer: "Due to smoking cigarettes 17.4 people die each year".
Pat: "How can point four of anybody die?".
Mike: "He means 17 die and four are on the point of dying".

100. INDICATOR STUCK

Pat was driving round and round the round-about when a Policeman stopped him and asked him the reason.

Pat replied, "I have just bought a new car and the indicator is stuck".

101. CAT MEAT

Woman: "Twenty tins of cat meat, please".

Grocer: "You must have a lot of cats".

Woman: "We don't have any cats. My husband likes cat meat in his lunch".

Grocer: "My dear woman, cat meat is not for human consumption. In fact, it could kill him".

Woman: "He has been eating it for a year and it hasn't done him any harm".

Grocer: "Well, he is your husband, so what he eats is your business".

The grocer didn't see her again for three months, then she came into the shop.

Grocer: "How is your husband these days?".

Woman: "Oh, he died last month".

Grocer: "I told you that the cat meat would kill him"

Woman: "It wasn't the cat meat that killed him. He broke his neck the night he fell off the yard wall."

102. DRINKING OUT OF SAUCER

Waitress: "Why do you drink your tea out of the saucer?".

Mike: "Because, when I drink it out of the cup, the spoon sticks in my eye".

103. NOSE IN POCKET

A man was assaulted and a fight developed. One man was taken to hospital because his ear had been bitten off.

Surgeon: "This is ridiculous in a civilised country; we shall have to notify the police. Do you think you would recognise the culprit again?".

Man: "I certainly would, for I have his nose in my pocket".

104. SENTENCED

Judge: "I find you guilty and I accordingly give you 14 days or £50".

Accused: If it is all the same to you, Guvenor, I'll take the £50".

105. STOLE TURKEY

Judge: "You are accused of stealing a turkey from Murphy's farm. Have you anything to say for yourself".

Accused: "I just took it for a lark, your Honour".

Judge: "You must have very poor eyesight if you took a turkey for a lark. I fine you £30".

106. ACQUITTED

The man was in Court charged with stealing a hen from his neighbour. His lawyer put up a good case for him and convinced the judge of his innocence.

Judge: "You are acquitted".

Man: "Does that mean I can keep the hen?".

107. HOPE IT IS BLOOD

The man had a bottle of whiskey in his hip-pocket as he ran for the Bus. He fell and felt something wet running down his leg. His comment was: "I hope it's blood".

108. FOUR YEARS BETWEEN

During the War a soldier looked very dejected after reading a letter from his wife.

Mate: "What are you looking so miserable for? Had you bad news from home?".

Soldier: "Yes, I have. My wife is expecting a baby".

Mate: "But that is good news".

Soldier: "No, it's not, for I haven't been home for two years".

Mate: "Cheer up! Two years are nothing. Sure there are four years between me and my brother".

109. GOLD SOVEREIGNS IN THE STREET

The Irishman heard the song in which it is said the streets of London are paved with gold coins. Being out of work, he went to London to try his luck. As soon as he came out of the railway station he was delighted to find a gold sovereign coin lying on the street. He quickly lifted it and was glad he came. He then noticed a blind man standing nearby begging with his little tin cup. The soft-hearted Irishman put the coin in the tin saying, "You take it, mate, I can see them and you can't".

110. LOOKING FOR BOOTS

During the First World War the soldier's boots had worn out and he was in dire need of a new pair.

Sergeant: "Go over the top and take a pair off a dead German. Don't be long until you are back".

Soldier: "Look, I managed to get a pair".

Sergeant: "Why did it take you so long?".

Soldier: "You know I have big feet. Well, I had to try about forty on before I got a pair to fit me".

111. IN THE DESERT

Three men were asked what they would like to take with them if they were to go into the Sahara Desert.

Englishman: "I would want a block of ice to keep me cool".

Scotsman: "I would take a case of Coke with me".

Irishman: "I would want a car door, so that I could screw down the window".

112. SAND AND CEMENT

On a building project two Irishmen accepted a labourer's job on the edge of the Sahara Desert. As soon as they alighted from the plane and saw all the sand, one exclaimed to the other: "Let's get out of here before the cement comes".

113. PULL THE FLEX BACK

The old lady had the phone installed in her home. The flex at the phone was too long for her liking, so she rang the operator and said, "The flex is too long at this end, please pull it back a bit at your end".

114. HENS STOPPED LAYING

Motorist: "Two of your hens have stopped laying".

Farmer's wife: "How do you know that?".

Motorist: "I have just run over two of them".

115. LORD MAYOR

Irishman: "Does your Lord Mayor, or Provost as you call him, wear a chain around his neck like our man does?".

Scotsman: "No, he just gangs aboot loose".

116. LADYSMITH
During the Boer War which took place in South Africa, a soldier wrote home to his wife, saying, "I'm making a shift for Ladysmith tomorrow".
"Good gracious", said the wife, "making a shift for Lady Smith and he couldn't even sew a button on his own shirt".

117. ANTIQUE DOOR
Antique dealer: "Madam, I see you are interested in that table. It belonged to Queen Anne."
Lady: "How do you know that?".
Dealer: "It says, 'Q.A.' on the leg. That is how I know".
Lady: "That is most interesting, for we have a door in our house which must have belonged to William the Conqueror".

118. MARRIED KANGAROO
Mary had gone to Australia and had written home to her Auntie, saying: "Auntie, I'm going to marry a native of Australia".
Later, her Aunt visited the Zoo and came to an enclosure where there was a Kangaroo. The plaque said, "native of Australia".
"My goodness," exclaimed the Aunt, "Is that what Mary has gone and married?".

119. FED HEN ON ICE
Pat had just returned from a job in Africa. He was asked if it was very hot there. He replied, "It sure was. In Africa we had to feed the hens on ice to prevent them laying boiled eggs".

120. HEART IN MOUTH
Traveller: "When I was in Timbuktu, a Brigand held me up. He fired his gun at me and the bullet hit me right here...", pointing to the left side of his chest.
Listener: "If the bullet had hit you there, you would be dead, for that is where your heart is".
Traveller: "Not that day, for then my heart was in my mouth".

121. BETTER AT THE REHEARSAL
Pat entered for the eating competition and won by a small margin.
Judge: "We congratulate you on your success".
Pat: "I don't understand why I didn't do better because I ate more at the

rehearsal this morning".

122. ATE CORNER OF MATTRESS
Pat had a bit of a nightmare and dreamt that he was eating shredded wheat. When he awoke in the morning he discovered that he had eaten the corner of his mattress.

123. BOY OR GIRL?
Neighbour: "Hello, Pat, I hear your sister has had a baby: her first, I believe. Is it a boy or a girl?".
Pat: "That's what is bothering me. I haven't heard, so I don't know whether I'm an Uncle or an Aunt".

124. SELLING A CAR
Pat: "I would like to sell my car, but it won't be easy, for it has 75,000 miles on it".
Barney: "Turn the clock back to 12,000 and it will sell well".
A month later -
Barney: "I see you haven't sold your car yet".
Pat: "No, I've decided to keep it, seeing it has only 12,000 miles done".

125. TOURNIQUET
Mike: "Pat, what's a tourniquet for?".
Pat: "It is something like a wedding ring: it is supposed to stop the circulation".

126. BARBER'S SHOP
The one-armed man went into the Barber's shop for a shave. He soon regretted it, for the barber cut him in quite a number of places.
Barber: "Were you ever in here before?".
Customer: "No, I lost my arm in the war".

127. CHRISTMAS CLUB
The Pub advertised its Christmas Club saying, "Pay what you like; get what you want".
Barney: "Pat, you only paid 50p and you demanded and got a bottle of whiskey because you argued that 'pay what you like; get what you want' entitled you to it. You should have seen the barman's face".

Pat: "I did see it, but it was nothing like what it was when I returned the bottle and asked for 10p on it".

128. HALF EXPECTING TRAIN
Tourist: "What is the idea of the Level Crossing gates being half open?"
Irish keeper: "Oh, that's because we are half expecting a train".

129. MOTOR RALLY
The Circuit of Ireland Motor Rally was in progress. As one car rounded a bend in the road they saw a tractor with two men in it, drive out of a field right into their path. To avoid crashing into it, they drove into the field where the tractor had just come out of.
One man in the tractor was heard to say to the other, "Boys, Paddy, we just got out of that field in time".

130. MOSS HOLE
Woman, coming running out of the peat moss: "Somebody come quickly, Pat, my husband, has fallen into a moss hole and the water is up to his ankles".
Neighbour: "If it is only up to his ankles, he will come to no harm".
Woman: "But he fell in head first".

131. SHOT TOE OFF
To give himself an added sense of security, the Irishman purchased a shot gun and kept it beside his bed at night. One night he saw something move at the foot of the bed. Before he realised what he was doing, he fired his gun, only to blow his big toe off. He was taken to hospital.
Doctor: "I'm sorry, Murphy, about your accident. It is a serious thing to lose a big toe".
Murphy: "Oh, that's all right, doctor. It could have been worse".
Doctor: "How could it have been worse?".
Murphy: "Well, I was thinking that if I had been lying the other way round in the bed, with my head at the foot of it, I might have blown my brains out".

132. STOPPED SMOKING
Warder to man in condemned cell: "Would you like a cigarette before they take you out to the gallows?".
Prisoner: "No, thanks, I'm trying to give up smoking".

133. CHIROPODIST

Pat's car had broken down by the roadside and another motorist kindly stopped and asked if he could help.

Pat: "Are you a mechanic, by any chance?".

Motorist: "No, I'm a Chiropodist".

Pat: "Then maybe you will give me a (toe) tow".

134. BON APPETITE

The Irishman on board ship found himself sitting beside a Frenchman at the lunch table.

Frenchman: "Bon appetite".

Irishman, reaching out his hand: "I'm Pat Murphy".

135. TICKET TO JEOPARDY

Pat called in at the local Travel Agency.

Agent: "Can I help you?".

Pat: "I would like a ticket to Jeopardy, please".

Agent: "I have never heard of such a place".

Pat: "That's very strange, for I have noticed a few Bill-boards which say, 'Thousands of jobs in jeopardy'".

136. BAKELITE

Teacher: "Now, children, in our English class today I want you to make up sentences. Someone give me a sentence with the word fascinate in it".

First pupil: "My Uncle has nine buttons on his waistcoat, but when he has a meal at our house he can only fascinate (fasten eight)".

Teacher: "Give me a sentence with the word centimetre in it".

Second pupil: "My wee sister doesn't like to come home from school alone, so sometimes I'm sent to meet her (centimetre)".

Teacher: "Give me a sentence with the word Bakelite in it".

Third pupil: "My grandfather has a long white beard and he smokes a pipe. Granny says if he is not careful he will set his bake a light (bakelite)".

137. WORM BY THE THROAT

Pat was having very little success with his fishing until a man suggested he steep his worms in whiskey to give them a bit of life.

Pat tried this and when he felt a tug at his line, he reeled it in only to find that the worm had a fish by the throat.

138. WHAT DO YOU CALL A FLEA?
"What do you call a flea in an Irishman's ear?".
Answer: "A space invader".

139. DRUNKS IN LONDON
Three Irishmen were taken to the police station in London for being drunk and disorderly.
Sergeant to first man: "What is your name?".
Man: "John".
Sergeant: "John what?".
Man, looking out of window: "John Collier".
Sergeant to second man: "What is your name?".
Man: "Mark".
Sergeant: "Mark what?".-
Man, glancing at shop sign: "Mark Spencer".
Sergeant to third man: "What is your name?".
Man: "Ken".
Sergeant: "Ken what?".
Man, glancing at shop sign: "Kentucky Fry".

140. FOREMAN'S BREATH
Pat had a steady job in the City's sewer, but he gave up the job. When asked, "Why give up the job?", he replied ,"I can't stand the foreman's breath."

141. A LA CARTE
The local Coalman spent a week-end in France and returned pretending he could speak French. He called with a customer and said, "How would you like your coal today...A La Carte or Cul de sac?".

142. MENTAL INSTITUTION
American: "We have buildings a hundred times larger than that one".
Pat: "That doesn't surprise me. That is a Mental Institution".

143. LOVE HER STILL
Pat: "She was only a Poteen maker's daughter, but I love her 'still'".

144. GUILLOTINE

The Englishman, the Scotsman and the Irishman were condemned to die by the Guillotine in France. The Englishman was called first, but the machine failed to work, so he was granted a reprieve. The same thing happened to the Scotsman and he was given a reprieve. The Irishman was called but before he put his head on the block, he looked up and said, "I know what's wrong with that Guillotine and he proceeded to tell them how to fix it!.

145. CLIMBED UP THE SPOUT (Drain Pipe)

The man asked his next door neighbour if he would look after his cat for him while he and his wife were on holiday.
Neighbour: "What would I have to do?".
Man: "Just put out a saucer of milk each morning and evening. We are very fond of the cat and would not like anything to happen to it".
Neighbour: "It won't be hard to put out the milk, so I'll do it".
Man: "Maybe you would keep an eye on Granny as she will be on her own".
Neighbour: "Certainly, we will keep a check on her".
Unfortunately, while they were away both the cat and Granny died.
Neighbour: "I'm sorry to tell you that the cat died while you were away".
Man: "That is bad news. It is a pity you didn't break the news gently to me for it has come as a great shock".
Neighbour: "How should I have told you?".
Man: "Well, you could have said, 'It climbed up the spout, walked along the roof to the end of it, fell off and broke its neck'. In that way I would have been prepared for the worst. By the way, how is Granny?".
Neighbour: "Well, she climbed up the spout, walked along the roof....", whereupon the man stopped him and said 'Say no more I know the worst'.

146. HURRICANE LAMP

The two men imbibed too much and when it was time for Pat to go home Barney told him to take the hurricane lamp to show him the way home. Pat returned the next day with the bird cage he had lifted by mistake.

147. LORRY DRIVER AND MONKEYS

The Zoo van broke down and the driver waved a lorry driver down.
Man: "I have two monkeys here: I'll give you £5 if you take them to the Zoo in Dublin".
Lorry Driver: "Certainly, I'll be glad to do so".

When the van driver eventually got to Dublin, he saw the lorry driver with the two monkeys.

Van driver: "I gave you £5 to take those two monkeys to the Dublin Zoo. Why did you not do as I asked?".

Lorry driver: "I did take them to the Zoo, but as there was some money left out of the £5, I thought I'd take them to the Cinema".

148. ORANGE AND GREEN BUDGIE

The Man had an orange coloured Budgie, so he bought a green one and put them into the same cage. Next morning the green one was lying dead and the orange one was in the corner of the cage with all his feathers gone.

Looking at his owner, he said, "Let me have another of his sort while I have my coat off".

(You can change the colours around to suit yourself)

149. KISSED THE BLARNEY STONE

Lady: "You certainly can talk; I'm afraid you kissed the Blarney stone".

Man: "To tell you the truth, I haven't, but I have kissed many a one who has!".

150. HORSE LOST ITS PETROL

A man on his horse rode into a modern town where few young people had ever seen a horse. He tethered the horse outside while he went into the Hotel. While he was inside, the horse relieved itself by emptying its bladder.

When the owner of the horse came out, one little boy said to him, "Mister, I hope you get home all right. While you were inside the Hotel, your horse lost all its petrol".

151. QUEEN VISITING HOSPITAL

Queen to patient: "Well, Sir, what is wrong with you?".

Patient: "I have a boil on my bum".

Matron after Queen had gone: "You should not have used that word to the Queen. You could have said you had a boil on your chest".

Princess Anne a week later: "My good man, what is wrong with you?"

Patient: "I have a boil on my chest".

Princess Anne:; "Oh, I see it has moved up a bit since my mother was here last week".

152. FLIES FIGHTING IN SOUP
Customer: "Waiter, there are two flies fighting in my soup".
Waiter: "Well, what about it: What do you want for 20p, a Bull Fight?".

153. O'REILLY?
Englishman: "My daughter has married an Irishman".
Friend: "Oh, really?".
Englishman: "No. O'Reilly".

154. WE CALL HIM 'GINGER'
A man walked into the Pub and asked, "Does George come in here?".
Man: "I don't know anyone by that name".
Man: "He had only one leg and one arm, do you not know him?".
Pat: I can't say I do".
Man: "By the way he is also bald. Well, not actually....he has one red hair sticking up".
Pat: Oh, I know who you mean now. We call him Ginger'".

155. SOMETHING I ATE
The American soldier returned to his old home in the Kentucky Mountains. Looking around the place, he said to his father, "Pa, that outside toilet hut is a disgrace. It must go".
Father: "We can't get rid of that. It is the only one we have".
The son took a hand grenade out of his pocket and threw it at the hut, blowing the whole thing to pieces.
Father: "Son, you shouldn't have done that, your granny was in that hut just now".
Just then granny's head popped up from behind a nearby bush and she exclaimed, "That could have killed me. It must have been something I ate!".

156. BURIED THE CAT
The arrogant visitor tried to make a fool of the Irish farmer.
Visitor: "You think you know a lot about farming. Well, last year I planted cabbages and what do you think came up?".
Farmer: "Cabbages, of course".
Visitor: "No Brussel Sprouts came up. Also, I planted radishes and what do you think came up?".
Farmer: "I don't know".

As the visitor walked away, feeling he had made a fool of the farmer, the farmer called him back.

Farmer: "Last year my cat died and I buried it. What do you think came up?".

Visitor: "I don't know".

Farmer: "Why of course, the Sanitary inspector came up, for it wasn't buried deep enough. Put that in your pipe and smoke it".

157. TWO FLIES IN THE SOUP

Customer: "What are these flies doing swimming in my soup?".

Waiter: "It looks to me as if they are doing the breast stroke".

158. BABY FLY

Neighbour fly: "How is baby fly these days?".

Mother fly: "Not too good. I had to walk the ceiling with him all last night".

159. MUSIC ON THE BRAIN

Boy: "My grandfather died with music on the brain".

Teacher: "I never heard of that before. How did it happen?".

Boy: "He was a furniture remover and a piano fell on his head".

160. STEAM ROLLER

The labourer on the building site was run over by a Steam Roller. The foreman told two of his men to take him home. On their return, he asked what the man's wife had to say.

Man: "She wasn't in when we called".

Foreman: "And what did you do with your mate?".

Man: "We pinned a note on his coat and slipped him under the door."

161. CHALK MARK ON THE WALL

Pat: "I'll meet you at the Town hall. If I'm there first I'll put a chalk mark on the wall, and if you are there first, you can rub it out".

162. WHERE DOES THIS ROAD GO?

Tourist: Where does this road go?".

Local: It doesn't go anywhere. I see it here every day".

163. WAITING FOR THE TRAIN

The woman had brought a new bed and she was paying for it weekly. When the "Tickman" called to collect the instalment, she had a complaint to make.

Woman: "There is something wrong with this bed for every time a train passes it would shake the life out of you. Come up and see for yourself.

Man (upstairs): "I see nothing wrong with the bed".

Woman: "Lie on top of it beside me and when the train passes soon you will see what I mean".

He obliged and lay down beside her. Just then her husband came in and bounded up the stairs. When he saw them both lying in bed, he said, "What is the meaning of all this?".

Debt Collector: "You won't believe it, but we are just waiting for a train to pass".

164. RUNNING AFTER BUS

A man was seen running after a bus. The conductor stopped the Bus, but the man refused to get on.

Man: "I'm running after the Bus in order to save 50p".

Conductor: "If that is so, then I suggest you run after a Taxi and save a couple of quid".

165. TWELFTH WEEK IN JULY

The Irishman wrote to a landlady in England asking for a booking for the twelfth week in July. The lady wrote back saying that in England, July had only four weeks.

166. SKELETON IN CUPBOARD

When a skeleton was found in a cupboard, a police enquiry was set in motion. They discovered that the skeleton belonged to the Irish Hide and Seek Champion who hadn't been heard of for some time.

167. BLACK MARIA

The Black Maria crashed into a Cement Mixer and the prisoners escaped. The Police are now looking for three hardened criminals.

168. 'WEE' SOLDIERS

A man who was only 4ft. 11 in. tried to join the Army. He was rejected because of his small stature. He couldn't understand it, because he had heard them singing, "Soldiers are we".

169. IRISHISMS
"Is that you standing there?".
"Are you not away home yet?".
"Excuse me, are you reading that paper you are sitting on?".

170. WOMAN IN BELFAST
Woman: "What was that terrible noise?".
Man: "It was a bomb going off".
Woman: "It had me scared at first, for I thought it was thunder and lightening".

171. AMERICAN BOASTING
The American was being shown around Belfast in a Taxi.
Driver: "That building is Queen's University".
American: "We could build that in two months".
Driver: "That building is our famous City Hall".
American: "We could build that in a month".
Driver: "That is Stormont, our parliament buildings".
American: "How long did it take to build that?".
Driver: "I don't know. It wasn't there last week when I was here".

172. INTENDED SUICIDE
First man: "Why have you that rope tied under your arms?".
Second man: "I want to hang myself, for I am tired of living".
First man: "You would need to put the rope around your neck".
Second man: "I tried that, but it nearly choked me".

173. HARDWARE SHOP
The Irishman in England was tired of being asked "Are you from Ireland".
He decided to attend an Elocution class to cover up his accent. Later, he walked into a shop and in a very polite accent asked for "A loaf, half a dozen eggs and a pound of bacon".
Shopkeeper: ""You're from Ireland, aren't you".
Man: "How did you know?".
Shopkeeper: "This is a hardware shop you are in".

174. SOLDIERS OUT LATE

Three soldiers were out late and tried to sneak past the guard.
Guard: "Who goes there?".
English man, mewed like a cat.
Guard: "Who goes there?".
Scotsman, mewed like a cat.
Guard: "Who goes there?".
Irishman: "It is another cat".

175. HEREAFTER

Caller at house: "Do you believe in the hereafter?".
Man, thinking it was the Elder from the Church said, "Yes, I do".
Caller: "Good, for I am here after the back rent".

176. BOY CRYING

Man: What are you crying for?"
Boy: "That man slapped me on the ear because Jimmy over there is smoking".
Man: "What has Jimmy smoking to do with you?".
Boy: "I set him alight".

177. THERMOMETER

Doctor to woman: "Put that thermometer in your mouth and do not speak until I tell you".
Husband: "Doctor, where can I buy one of those things".

178: DEATH NOTICES

Old Johnny Brown reads the paper in bed every morning. He looks at the death notices and if his name is not there, then he gets up .

179. HOLE IN THE HEART

The man taken to hospital after complaining about pains in his chest. The first X-Ray revealed that he had a hole in the heart. His wife was greatly upset, but equally relieved the next day when told that a second X-Ray had discovered that he had a polo mint in his shirt pocket and that he could go home.

180. CHEESE IN HIS "PIECE"
The man looked at his "piece", saw cheese in it and threw it away. For three days he did this.

Man: "If you don't like cheese why don't you get your wife to put something else in it?".

Mate: "My wife is in hospital and I make my own lunch up".

181. HAND-GLIDING
The man was sent to prison for hand-gliding. A policeman caught him gliding his hand into a woman's handbag.

182. STEAMROLLER ACCIDENT
Barney: "I hear old Pat is dead. What happened him?".

Mike: "A steamroller ran over him and crushed his finger".

Barney: "How could that kill him?".

Mike: "Unfortunately, he was scratching his nose at the time".

183. TWINS AND SHOT GUN
Friend: "Pat, where are you going with that shot gun?".

Pat: "My wife has just had twins and I'm going looking for the man who was responsible for the second child".

184. GREEN BLACKBERRIES
Pat was showing a friend around his garden.

Friend: "What are those berries?".

Pat: "They are blackberries".

Friend: "They look red to me".

Pat: "Yes, blackberries are red when they are green".

185. ACCUSED OF ADULTERY
An Irish woman went to a Solicitor and suggested that proceedings be taken out with regards to her husband having committed adultery.

Solicitor: "Tell me, what evidence have you of your husband having committed adultery?".

Woman: "I am convinced that he is not the father of my second child".

186. TIE SIZE
Woman to shop assistant: "I wonder if you can help me. My husband asked

me to get him a tie, but I forgot to ask him what size he wears".

187. NEWS ALERT
Reporter: "Two convicts escaped from the local prison this morning. One is 6ft. 6 inches tall and the other is 4 ft. 9 inches tall. The Police are looking high and low for them."

188. BUYING A WIG
Shop Assistant: "That wig will cost you £25 plus tax."
Man: "I don't want the tacks. Glue will be more comfortable."

189. JAIL ESCAPER
Cook to Prison Warder: "Watch out for Murphy tomorrow."
Warder: "Why?"
Cook" "Because he has asked for a packed lunch tomorrow."

190. ABSTAIN FROM DRINK
Lecturer at meeting: "I want to show you what strong drink can do. Here are two glasses; in one is water and in the other whiskey. Watch carefully as I put this worm into the glass of water. You will notice that it wriggles about and is very much alive. Now watch as I put it into the glass of Whiskey. It dies even before it hits the bottom. Now what is the moral of the illustration?"
Little man with red nose: "It means that if you don't want worms you should drink Whiskey."

191. AIRPORT SIGN
Walking along the road an old lady saw a sign which read, 'Airport 5 miles'." Turning to her companion she was heard to remark: "How could any pilot see that sign from far away up there?"

192. SKATING ON ICE
The Irishman had learned to ice skate and decided to enter a competition to represent his country. As the other contestants watched their scores, the results were reasonable. When the Irishman took to the ice, he kept falling all over the place. The other Markers gave him practically nothing. However, the Marker from Ireland gave him full marks. When asked why

he did so, he replied, "Sure you know its very slippery out there."

193. GATHERING LEAVES
Woman to friend: "My husband's new job has landed him in hospital."
Friend: "What happened?"
Woman: "He was told to gather leaves in the Park for the Council and he fell out of the tree on his first day."

194. DECORATED
Did you hear about the soldier who came out of Buckingham Palace all covered in wall paper? He had just been decorated!

NUMBERING SYSTEM

The numbers of the jokes and stories in each
chapter follow on from their respective numbers
in Volume One of Joe's Jokes. Thus in Chapter
One Volume One the Tales about Clergymen run
from 1 to 70, therefore in Volume Two the first
tale in that chapter begins with No.71